THE REAL GLADSTONE: AN ANE(

BY

J. Ewing Ritchie

THE REAL GLADSTONE: AN ANECDOTAL BIOGRAPHY

Published by Wallachia Publishers

New York City, NY

First published circa 1898

Copyright © Wallachia Publishers, 2015

All rights reserved

ABOUT WALLACHIA PUBLISHERS

<u>Wallachia Publishers</u> mission is to publish the world's finest European history texts. More information on our recent publications and catalog can be found on our website.

PREFACE.

In this little work I have aimed to write, not a history or a biography, not a criticism or a eulogy, but merely to give a few scattered notes, gathered from many quarters, for the general public, rather than for the professional politician. Lord Rosebery is reported to have said that it will require many writers to give a complete biography of Mr. Gladstone. He may be right; but the evil of it will be, the work, if exhaustive, will be exhausting. Especially will it be so in these busy times, when yesterday's biographies become stale to a public forgetful of the past, caring only for the present, oblivious of the morrow. It is almost an impertinence to speak of the many claims Mr. Gladstone has on a people whom he has served so long. All I claim to do is to give a few data which may help them to estimate the

in short, more or less imperfectly, 'The Real Gladstone.'

Clacton,

CHAPTER I. BIRTH AND SCHOOLDAYS.

Many, many years ago England's foremost statesman, as George Canning then was, distrusted by the multitude, feared by his colleagues, regarded with suspicion by the First Gentleman of the Age—as it was the fashion to term George the Magnificent, who was then seated on the British throne—wearied of the strife and turmoil of party, spent a short time at Seaforth House, bidding what he deemed his farewell to his Liverpool correspondents. His custom, we are told, was to sit for hours gazing on the wide expanse of waters before him. His had been a marvellous career. Born out of the circle of the ruling classes, by his indomitable energy, the greatness of his intellectual gifts, his brilliant eloquence, he had lifted himself up above his contemporaries, and had become their leader; and here he was about to quit the scene of his triumphs—to reign as Viceroy in a far-off land. Canning, however, did not retire from the Parliamentary arena, but stopped at home to be Premier of Great Britain and Ireland, and to let all Europe know that this country had done with the Holy Alliance; that a new and better spirit was walking the earth; that the dark night of bigotry was past, and that the dawn of a better day had come. As he sat there looking out over the waters, a little one was to be seen playing below upon the sand. That little lad was the son of Canning's host and friend, and his name was William Ewart Gladstone. Does it not seem as if the little one playing on the sand had unconsciously caught something of the genius, of the individuality, of the eloquence, of the loftiness of aim, of the statesman who sat above him overlooking the sea? Circumstances have much to do with the formation of character. To the youthful Gladstone, Canning was a light, a glory, and a star.

William Ewart Gladstone was born on December 29, 1809, at a house which may still be seen, 62, Rodney Street, Liverpool. He was of Scotch extraction, his father, a Liverpool merchant, having an estate in Scotland. Mr. Gladstone senior lived to become one of the merchant princes of Great Britain, a Baronet, and a Member of Parliament. He died, at the advanced age of eighty-seven, in 1851. His wife was Anne, daughter of Andrew Robertson, of Stornoway. They had six children; William Ewart Gladstone was the third. The family were all brought up as debaters. The children and their parents are said to have argued upon everything. They would debate whether the meat should be boiled or broiled, whether a window should be shut or opened, and whether it was likely to be fine or wet next day.

As a little boy, Gladstone went to school at Seaforth, where the late Dean Stanley was a pupil. The latter is responsible for the following: 'There is a small school near Liverpool at which Mr. Gladstone was brought up before he went to Eton. A few years ago, another little boy who was sent to this school, and whose name I will not mention, called upon the old clergyman who was the headmaster. The boy was now a young man, and he said to the old clergyman: "There is one thing in which I have never in the least degree improved since I was at school—the casting up of figures." "Well," replied the master, "it is very extraordinary that it should be so, because certainly no one could be a more incapable arithmetician at school than you were; but I will tell you a curious thing. When Mr. Gladstone was at the school, he was just as incapable at addition and subtraction as you were; now you see what he has become—he is one of the greatest of our financiers.'"

William Gladstone left home for Eton after the summer holidays of 1821, the headmaster being Dr. Keate. Sir Roderick Murchison describes him as 'the prettiest little boy that ever went to Eton.' From the first he was a hard student and well behaved, and exercised a good influence over his schoolfellows. 'I was a thoroughly idle boy,' said the late Bishop Hamilton of Salisbury, 'but I was saved from worse things by getting to know Gladstone.' Another schoolfellow remembered how he turned his glass upside down, and refused to drink a coarse toast proposed according to custom at an election dinner. His most intimate friend was Arthur Hallam, of whom he wrote an article in the Daily Telegraph, which created universal admiration. He had the courage of his opinions, and when bantered by some of his associates for his interfering on behalf of some ill-used pigs, he offered to write his reply 'in good round hand upon their faces.' He took no delight in games, but kept a private boat for his own use, and was a great walker with his select friends. He was accustomed on holidays to go as far as Salt Hall, to bully the fat waiter, eat toasted cheese, and drink egg-wine—hence he seems to have been familiarly known as Mr. Tipple. But he soon became especially distinguished by his editing the Eton Miscellany, and for his skill in debate at what was commonly called the Pop. Its meetings were generally held over a cook-shop, and its politics were intensely Tory, though current politics were forbidden subjects. His maiden speech was in favour of education. Eton at that time was not a good school, writes Sir Francis Doyle; but he testifies strongly to the virtues of the debating society. He continues: 'In the debating society Mr. Gladstone soon distinguished himself. I had the privilege of listening to his maiden speech. It began, I recollect, with these words: "Sir, in this age of increasing and still increasing civilization . . ." After Mr. Gladstone's arrival, the debating society doubled and trebled itself in point of numbers, and the discussions became much fuller of interest and animation. Hallam and Mr. Gladstone took the lead.' Not content with the regular debating society, Mr. Gladstone and a few others, such as Miles Gaskell and Canning, established an inner one, held on certain summer afternoons in the garden of one Trotman. Sir Francis continues: 'It happened that my tutor, Mr. Okes, rented a small garden at the rear of Trotman's, and by some chance found himself there on the occasion of one of these debates. To his surprise, he heard three or four boys on the other side of the wall sneering, shouting, and boohooing in the most unaccountable manner. There seemed but one conclusion to him as an experienced Eton tutor—viz., that they were what we at the Custom-House used somewhat euphemistically to term under the influence of liquor. He thereupon summoned Mr. Gladstone to his study, listened gloomily and reluctantly to his explanations and excuses, and all but handed over our illustrious Premier, with his subordinate orators, to be flogged for drunkenness.'

Dr. Wilkinson, in his 'Reminiscences of Eton,' gives a couplet and its translation by Mr. Gladstone, when a boy at Eton:

As to the Miscellany, with which Mr. Gladstone had so much to do, Sir Francis continues: 'It would have fallen to the ground but for Mr. Gladstone's energy, perseverance, and tact. I may as well remark here that my father—as I have said elsewhere, a man of great ability as well as of great experience in life—predicted Mr. Gladstone's future eminence from the manner in which he handled this somewhat tiresome business. "It is not," he remarked, "that I think his papers better than yours or Hallam's—that is not my meaning at all; but the force of character he has shown in managing his subordinates (insubordinates I should rather call them), and the combination of ability and power that he has made evident, convince me that such a young man cannot fail to distinguish himself hereafter.'" Further, Sir Francis Doyle writes: 'I cannot take leave of Mr. Gladstone's Eton career without recording a joke of his which, even in this distance of time, seems calculated to thrill the heart of Midlothian with horror and dismay. He was then, I must remind my hearers, a high Tory, and, moreover, used to criticise my passion for the turf. One day I was steadily computing the odds for the Derby, as they stood in a morning newspaper. Now, it happened that the Duke of Grafton owned a colt called Hampden, who figured in the aforesaid list. "Well," cried Mr. Gladstone, reading off the odds, "Hampden, at any rate, I see, is in his proper place between Zeal and Lunacy!"'

The impression Gladstone made on his schoolfellows at Eton is clearly shown in a letter of Miles Gaskell to his mother, pleading for his going to Oxford rather than Cambridge: 'Gladstone is no ordinary individual. . . . If you finally decide in favour of Cambridge, my separation from Gladstone will be a source of great sorrow to me.' And Arthur Hallam wrote: 'Whatever may be our lot, I am very confident that he is a bud that will blossom with a richer fragrance than almost any whose early promise I have witnessed.'

Gladstone, as has already been shown, was one of the principal members of the staff of the Eton Miscellany. He was then seventeen, and in one of the articles signed by him he expressed his fear that he would not be able to direct public opinion into the right channel. He was aware that merit was always rewarded, but he asked himself if he possessed that merit. He dared not presume that he did possess it, though he felt within him a something which made him hope to be able, without much hindrance, to gain public favour, and, as Virgil said, 'celerare viam rumore secundo.' We find Gladstone the Etonian expressing similar hopes in an article on 'Eloquence.' The young author shows us himself and his school-colleagues fascinated by the resounding debates in the House of Commons, and dreaming, boy-like, of making a successful Parliamentary début, perhaps being offered a Government berth—a Secretaryship of State, even the post of Prime Minister. While entertaining these ambitious views Mr. Gladstone calmed his mind by 'taking to poetry.' Several poetical pieces, including some verses on 'Richard Cœur-de-Lion,' and an ode to 'The Shade of Wat Tyler,' date from this period.

As a pendant to this fragmentary sketch of Mr. Gladstone's schooldays, we may quote the lively description of the young editor given by Sir Francis Doyle in 'A Familiar Epistle to W. E. Gladstone, Esq., M.P.,' published in 1841. Sir Francis paints a delightful picture of the rédacteur-en-chef:

Dr. Furnivall, president of the Maurice Rowing Club, lately sent Mr. Gladstone a copy of his letter on 'Sculls or Oars.' The ex-Prime Minister, in returning his thanks for the letter, says: 'When I was at Eton, and during the season, I sculled constantly, more than almost any other boy in the school. Our boats then were not so light as they now are, but they went along merrily, with no fear of getting them under water.'

CHAPTER II. GLADSTONE AT OXFORD.

After spending six months with private tutors, in October, 1828, he went up to Christ Church, Oxford, and the following year was nominated to a studentship. 'As for Gladstone,' writes Sir Francis Doyle, 'in the earlier part of his undergraduateship he read steadily, and did not exert himself to shine as a speaker; in point of fact, he did not attempt to distinguish himself in the Debating Society till he had pretty well made sure of his distinction in the Schools. I used often to walk with him in the afternoon, but I never recollect riding or boating in his company, and I believe that he was seldom diverted from his normal constitutional between two and five along one of the Oxford roads. The most adventurous thing I ever did at Oxford in Mr. Gladstone's company, if it really were as adventurous as I find he still asserts it to have been, was when I allowed myself to be taken to Dissenting chapels. We were rewarded by hearing Dr. Chalmers preach on two occasions, and Rowland Hill at another time.'

Gladstone seems to have delighted in these escapades. His mother was an occasional attendant on the ministrations of the celebrated Dissenting preacher Dr. Raffles, of Liverpool, and possibly might have taken the future Premier with her. His attendance at church was very regular. 'He used rather to mount guard over my religious observances,' writes Sir Francis Doyle, 'and habitually marched me off after luncheon to the University sermon at two o'clock. Now, I have not the gift of snoring comfortably under a dull preacher; instead of a narcotic he acts on my nerves as an irritant, but with Mr. Gladstone the case was different. One afternoon I looked up, and discovered, not without a glow of triumph, that although the reverend gentleman above me had not yet arrived at his "Thirdly," my Mentor was sleeping the sleep of the just. "Hullo!" said I to myself, "no more two-o'clock sermons for me." Accordingly, on the very next occasion when he came to carry me off, my answer was ready: "No, thank you, not to-day. I can sleep just as well in my arm-chair as at St. Mary's." The great man was discomfited, and retired, shaking his head, but he acknowledged his defeat by troubling me no more in that matter.'

Cardinal Manning had been the principal leader in the Oxford Debating Society till Mr. Gladstone appeared upon the scene. At once he and Gaskell became the leading Christ Church orators, and the great oratorical event of the time was Mr. Gladstone's speech against the first Reform Bill. 'Most of the speakers,' writes Sir Francis Doyle, who was present on the occasion, 'rose more or less above their ordinary level, but when Mr. Gladstone sat down we all of us felt that an epoch in our lives had arrived. It was certainly the finest speech of his that I ever heard. The effect produced by that great speech led to his being returned to Parliament as M.P. for Newark by the Tory Duke of Newcastle, who is remembered for his question, "May I not do what I like with my own?"'

To return to Mr. Gladstone's career at the University. In 1831 he took a double first-class, and would easily have attained a Fellowship in any college where Fellowships depended upon a competitive examination. He held with Scott, the foremost scholar of the day, the second place in the Ireland for 1829. In that year a deputation from the Union of Cambridge went to Oxford to take part in a debate on the respective merits of Byron and Shelley. One of the Cambridge party was Monckton Milnes, afterwards Lord Houghton. He writes: 'The man that took me most was the youngest Gladstone, of Liverpool—I am sure a very superior person.' On all he seems to have exercised a beneficial influence. He deprecated the example of the gentlemen commoners, and did much to check the pernicious habit prevalent at that time in the University, of over-indulgence in wine. His tutor was the Rev. Robert Briscoe. He also attended the lectures of the Rev. Dr. Benton on divinity and Dr. Pusey on Hebrew. He read classics privately with a tutor of the Bishop of St. Andrews. In 1830 he was at Cuddesdon Vicarage with a small reading-party, where he seems to have mastered Hooker's 'Ecclesiastical Polity.' He founded and presided over an essay society called after his name, of which he was successively secretary and president. In his maiden speech at the Union in 1830 he defended Catholic emancipation; declared the Duke of Wellington's Government unworthy of the confidence of the nation; opposed the removal of Jewish disabilities; and argued for the gradual emancipation of slavery rather than immediate abolition.

It is evident that all the time of his University career Mr. Gladstone had a profoundly religious bias, and at one time seems to have contemplated taking Holy Orders. Bishop Wordsworth declared that no man of his standing read the Bible more or knew it better. One of his fellow-students writes: 'Poor Gladstone mixed himself up with the St. Mary Hall and Oriel set, who are really for the most part only fit to live with maiden aunts and keep tame rabbits.' At this time Mr. Gladstone's High Churchmanship does not seem to have been so pronounced as it afterwards became. He was a disciple of Canning, and rejoiced at Catholic emancipation. 'When in Scotland, staying at his father's house in Kincardineshire, he attended the Presbyterian Kirk zealously and contentedly, and took me with him,' writes Sir Francis Doyle, 'to what they call the "fencing of the tables," an operation lasting five or six hours.'

One of Gladstone's college acquaintances was Martin Tupper, whose 'Proverbial Philosophy' had a sale out of all proportion to its merits, in 1864. He wrote—

'My first acquaintance with Gladstone,' Martin Tupper writes, 'was a memorable event. It was at that time not so common a thing for undergraduates to go to the Communion at Christ Church Cathedral, that holy celebration being supposed to be for the particular benefit of Deans and Canons and Masters of Arts; so when two undergraduates went out of the chancel together after Communion, which they had both attended, it is small wonder that they addressed each other genially, in defiance of Oxford etiquette, nor that a friendship so well begun has continued to this hour.' He testifies how Gladstone was the foremost man—warm-hearted, earnest, hard working, and religious, and had a following even in his teens.

The following anecdote is amusing. Tupper writes: 'I had the honour at Christ Church of being prize-taker of Dr. Benton's theological essay, "The Reconciliation of Matthew and John," when Gladstone, who had also contested it, stood second, and when Dr. Benton had me before him to give me the twenty-five pounds' worth of books, he requested me to allow Mr. Gladstone to have five pounds' worth, as he was so good a second.' Alas! Mr. Tupper in after-life was led to think that the man to whom at one time he looked up, had deviated from the proper path. In his 'Three Hundred Sonnets,' he kindly undertook, in the reference to Gladstone, to warn the public to

And again he wrote of a

Still, it is well to quote in this connection how Tupper considered Gladstone the central figure at Oxford University. He writes: 'Fifty years ago Briscoe's Aristotle class at Christ Church was comprised almost wholly of men who have since become celebrated, some in a remarkable degree; and as we believe that so many names afterwards attaining to great distinction have rarely been associated at one lecture board, either at Oxford or elsewhere, it may be allowed to one who counts himself the least and lowest of the company to pen this brief note of those old Aristotelians. In this class was Gladstone, ever from youth up the beloved and admired of many personal intimates.'

Miss Clough's character of Gladstone, solely from his handwriting, is thus recorded by Lord Houghton: 'A well-judging person; a good classic; considerate; apt to mistrust himself; undecided; if to choose a profession, would prefer the Church; has much application; a good reasoner; very affectionate and tender in his domestic relations; has a good deal of pride and determination, or rather obstinacy; is very fond of society, particularly ladies'; is neat, and fond of reading.'

Bishop Wordsworth writes: 'My cousin William Wordsworth, then living at Eton, was dining at Liverpool at the house of a great Liverpool merchant just after Gladstone had taken his degree. Amongst the company were Wordsworth, the poet, and Mr. John Gladstone, the father of the future Premier. After dinner, the poet congratulated the father on the success of his distinguished son. "Yes, sir," replied the father, "I thank you. My son has greatly distinguished himself at the University, and I trust he will continue to do so when he enters public life, for there is no doubt that he is a man of great ability, but he has no stability."'

Sir Francis Doyle describes a visit he paid to Gladstone at his father's house. 'Whilst there,' he writes, 'I was very much struck with the remarkable acuteness and great natural powers of Mr. Gladstone the father. Under his influence, apparently, nothing was taken for granted between the father and his sons. A succession of arguments on great topics and small topics alike— arguments conducted with perfect good humour, but also with the most implacable logic— formed the staple of the family conversations. Hence, it was easy to see from what foundations Mr. Gladstone's skill as a debater was built up.' Further illustrative traits are supplied. For instance, one of the amusements of the place was shooting with bows and arrows. The arrows were lost in the long grass; Sir Francis would have left them to chance and time. Not so Mr. Gladstone. He insisted on their being all found. Again, on a trip to Dunottar Castle, Mr. Gladstone was riding a skittish chestnut mare, who would not let him open a gate in front of him. 'My cob,' Sir Francis writes, 'was perfectly docile, and quiet as a sheep. I naturally said, "Let me do that for you." But no; his antagonist had to be tamed, but it took forty minutes to do so, and then the horsemen proceeded on their way.' It is said that Mr. Rarey, the horse-tamer, subsequently had a high opinion of Mr. Gladstone's skill as an equestrian.

CHAPTER III. ENTERS PARLIAMENT.

In 1832 Mr. Gladstone left Oxford, and after spending six months in Italy, he was recalled to England to become Member for Newark. In his address he declared that the duties of governors are strictly and peculiarly religious, and that legislators, like individuals, are bound to carry throughout their acts the spirit of the high truths they have acknowledged. Much required to be done for popular education, and labour should receive adequate remuneration. He regarded slavery as sanctioned by Holy Scripture, but he was in favour of the gradual education and emancipation of the slaves. It was said that he was the Duke of Newcastle's nominee. He replied that he was nothing of the kind—that he came there by the invitation of the Red Club, than whom none were more respectable and intelligent. He was returned at the head of the poll. Newark rejoiced in two members. Another Tory was second, and the Liberal candidate, Serjeant Wilde, was defeated. Mr. Gladstone accordingly took his seat in the first Reformed Parliament, which met in January, 1833. His maiden speech was on the Anti-slavery Debate, to defend his father from an attack made on him by Lord Howick with regard to the treatment of his slaves in Demerara. On the morning of the debate, as he was riding in Hyde Park, a passer-by pointed him out to another new member, Lord Charles Russell, and said, 'That is Gladstone; he is to make his maiden speech to-night; that will be worth hearing.'

Commenting on Mr. Disraeli's début in the House of Commons, Professor Prynne writes: 'This was a contrast to the graceful, harmonious, almost timid, maiden speech of Mr. W. E. Gladstone—a manner that I never saw equalled, except by Lord Derby when he was in the House of Commons. The speaking of these two was like a stream pouring foam, or it may be described as reading from a book. Of Mr. Gladstone we all agreed in saying, "This is a young man of great promise."' A foreigner writes that until he had heard Mr. Gladstone speak he never believed that the English was a musical language, but that after hearing him he was convinced that it was the most melodious of living tongues.

About this time there appeared Mr. James Grant's 'Random Recollections.' It is amusing to read: 'I have no idea that he will ever acquire the reputation of a great statesman. His views are not sufficiently enlarged or profound for that; his celebrity in the House of Commons will chiefly depend on his readiness and dexterity as a clever debater, in conjunction with the excellence of his elocution and the gracefulness of his manner when speaking.' 'When a Select Committee of the House of Commons,' writes Sir George Stephen, 'was appointed to take evidence on the working of the apprenticeship system among the West Indian blacks, it was arranged between Buxton on the one side and Gladstone on the other that Mr. Burge and myself should be admitted as their respective legal advisers. At that time evidently Mr. Gladstone had been recognised as the champion of the one party as much as Mr. Buxton of the other.'

In the anti-slavery recollections of Sir George Stephen we have a graphic account of the struggle between Gladstone, as the advocate of slavery, and Sir John Jerome, a colonial judge, who may be said to have died a martyr to his anti-slavery zeal. 'I shall never forget,' writes Sir George, 'his examination before the Apprenticeship Committee. Gladstone employed all his ingenuity in vain, and no man has a greater share of logical acumen, to bewilder him. But Jerome was quite his match. His evidence was argumentative, and therefore the cross-examination was in the nature of argument, as it generally is in Parliamentary Committees. It was a brilliant affair of thrust and counter-thrust. Gladstone was calm, imperturbable, and deliberate; Jerome wide-awake, ready at every point, and, though full of vivacity, as impossible to catch tripping as a French rope-dancer. He evaded what he could not answer, but evaded it so adroitly that Gladstone might detect but could not expose the evasion; and every now and then Jerome retorted objection to objection with a readiness that made it difficult to say which was the examiner and which the examined. The rest of the Committee silently watched the scene, as a conflict between two practised intellectual gladiators, and I am persuaded that Mr. Gladstone himself would admit that Jerome had not the worst of it. But if Mr. Gladstone had studied in the school of Oxford, Jerome was educated as an advocate for the French Bar, so they met on equal terms, while Jerome had the advantage of a good cause.'

Mr. Gladstone has been celebrated for his explanations. One of the earliest of them was written when he was Conservative candidate for Newark, addressed to a Mr. John Simpson, a Conservative Nonconformist. It is dated 'Hawarden, Chester, July 10, 1841.'

In Parliament Mr. Gladstone defended the Irish Church, and when in the next session Mr. Hume introduced a Universities' Admission Bill, intended to enable Dissenters to attend the Universities, Mr. Gladstone strongly opposed it. Soon after came the Tory reaction, and a General Election, at which Mr. Gladstone was again returned for Newark, in conjunction, however, this time with Serjeant Wilde. The new Parliament met in February, 1835. Mr. Gladstone was then Junior Lord of the Treasury in the new Government formed by Sir Robert Peel, a Government of but very short duration. Sir Francis Doyle writes: 'When Mr. Gladstone had established himself as a rising M.P. at the Albany, he breakfasted there, and met the poet Wordsworth. The great poet sat in state surrounded by young and enthusiastic admirers. His conversation was very like the "Excursion," turned into vigorous prose.' At this time Wilberforce, afterwards Bishop of Oxford and Winchester, wrote to him: 'It would be affectation in you, which you are above, not to know that few young men have the weight you have in the House of Commons, and are gaining rapidly through the country. Now, I do not urge you to consider this as a talent for the use of which you must render an account, for so I know you do esteem it, but what I want to urge upon you is that you should calmly look before you—see the degree of weight and influence to which you may fairly, if God spares your life and powers, look forward in future years, and thus act now with a view to then. There is no height to which you may not fairly rise in this country.' Mr. Gladstone's reply was not that of an optimist: 'The principles of civil government have decayed amongst us as much as I suspect those which are ecclesiastical, and one does not see an equally ready or sure provision for their revival. One sees in actual existence the apparatus by which our institutions are to be threatened and the very groundwork of the national character is to be broken up; but on the other hand, if we look around for the masses of principle—I mean of enlightened principle blended with courage and devotion, which are the human means of resistance—these I feel have yet to be organized, almost created.'

In July, 1838, Mr. W. E. Gladstone wrote to Mr. Murray, the publisher, from 6, Carlton Gardens, informing him that he has written and thinks of publishing some papers on the relationship of the Church and the State, which would probably fill a moderate octavo volume, and he would be glad to know if Mr. Murray would be inclined to see them. Mr. Murray saw the papers, and on August 9 he agreed with Mr. Gladstone to publish 750 or 1,000 copies of the work on Church and State on half-profits, the copyright to remain with the author after the first edition was sold. The work was immediately sent to press, and proofs were sent to Mr. Gladstone, about to embark for Holland. A note was received from the author, dated from Rotterdam, saying that sea-sickness prevented him from correcting the proofs on the passage. This was Mr. Gladstone's first appearance as author, and the work proved remarkably successful.

On receiving a copy of the book Sir Robert Peel exclaimed: 'With such a career before him, why should he write books?' In other quarters the book met with a warmer appreciation. Baron Bunsen wrote: 'It is the book of the times—a great event—the first since Burke that goes to the bottom of the question, far above his party and his times. I sat up till after midnight, and this morning I continued till I had read the whole. Gladstone is the first man in England as to intellectual power, and he has heard higher tones than anyone else in this land.' Dr. Arnold was delighted with it. Newman says to a friend: 'Gladstone's book, you see, is making a sensation.' Again he writes: 'The Times is again at poor Gladstone; really, I feel as if I could do anything for him. I have not read his book, but its consequences speak for it. Poor fellow! it is so noble a thing.'

Sir Henry Taylor wrote: 'I am reading Gladstone's book, which I shall send you, if he has not. It is closely and deeply argumentative, perhaps too much in the nature of a series of profound corollaries for a book which takes so very demonstrative a character, leaves one to expect what is impossible, and to feel drawn on by a postulate; but it is most able and profound, and written in language which cannot be excelled for clearness. It is too philosophical to be generally read, but it will raise his reputation in the opinion of those who do read it, and will not embarrass him so much in political life as a popular quotable book on such subjects might be apt to do. His party speak of him as the man who will be one day at their head, and certainly no man of his standing has yet appeared who seems likely to stand in his way. Two wants, however, may lie across his political career—want of robust health and want of flexibility.'

Writing to Mr. John Murray, Lord Mahon, afterwards Lord Stanhope, says: 'Mr. Gladstone's volume has lately engaged much of my attention. It is difficult to feel quite free from partiality where so amiable and excellent a man is concerned; but if my friendship does not blind me, I should pronounce his production as marked by profound ecclesiastical learning and eminent native ability. At the same time, I must confess myself startled at some of his tenets; his doctrine of Private Judgment especially seems to me a contradiction in terms, attempting to blend together the incompatible advantages of the Romanists and of the Protestant principle upon that point.'

Two years afterwards, we find a reference to the same subject. 'As to the third edition of "The State in its Relations to the Church," I should think the remaining copies had better be got rid of in whatever summary or ignominious mode you may deem best. They must be dead beyond recall. . . . With regard to the fourth edition, I do not know whether it would be well to procure any review or notice of it, and I am not a fair judge of its merits, even in comparison with the original form of the work; but my idea is that it is less defective, both in the theoretical and historical development, and ought to be worthy of the notice of those who deemed the earlier editions worth their notice and purchase; that it really would put a reader in possession of the view it was intended to convey, which, I fear, is more than can be said of any of its predecessors.'

Mr. Murray does not seem to have had many letters from Mr. Gladstone, though Croker mentions his having called on Mr. Murray to express his dissatisfaction on an article which appeared in the Quarterly on the Corn Laws. When, in 1843, the Copyright Bill was the subject of legislation, he wrote to Mr. Murray: 'I cannot omit to state that I learn from your note that steps are being taken here to back the recent proceedings of the Legislature. I must not hesitate to express my conviction that what Parliament has done will be fruitless unless the law be seconded by the adoption of such modes of publication as will allow the public here and in the colonies to obtain possession of new and popular English works at moderate prices, if it be practicable for authors and publishers to make such arrangements, I should hope to see a great extension of our book trade, as well as much advantage to literature from the measures that have now been taken, and from those which I trust we shall be enabled to take in completion of them. But unless the proceedings of the trade itself adapt and adjust themselves to the altered circumstances, I can feel no doubt that we shall relapse into or towards the old state of things— the law will be first evaded and then relaxed.' This sensible hint of Mr. Gladstone's does not seem to have been entirely thrown away—at any rate, as far as Mr. Murray was concerned.

About the same time Mr. Gladstone seems to have been not a little moved by our military proceedings in India. When Lieutenant Eyre's 'Military Operations in Cabool' appeared, Mr. Murray sent Mr. Gladstone a copy. He replied: 'I have read it with great pain and shame, which are, I fear, as one must say in such a case, the tests of its merits as a work. May another occasion for such a narrative never arise!' A humane wish, as subsequent events show, not likely to be speedily realized.

'Church and State' soon reached a third edition, and led to the famous review of it by Macaulay, in which he speaks of Gladstone as 'the rising hope of the stern and unbending Tories.' 'I have bought Gladstone's book on Church and State,' he writes to Macvey Napier, 'and I think I can make a good article on it. It seems to me the very thing for a spirited, popular, and at the same time gentlemanlike, critique.' Again he writes: 'I met Gladstone at Rome. We talked and walked together in St. Peter's during the best part of an afternoon, and I have in consequence been more civil to him personally than I otherwise should have been. He is both a clever and an able man, with all his fanaticism.' At this time Gladstone's eyesight failed him, and the doctors recommended him to spend the winter at Rome, where he met, besides Macaulay, Henry Manning and Cardinal Wiseman and Grant, who afterwards became Roman Catholic Bishop of Southwark. Among the visitors at Rome that winter were the widow and daughters of Sir Stephen Richard Glynne, of Hawarden Castle, Flintshire. Mr. Gladstone was already acquainted with these ladies, having been a friend of Lady Glynne's eldest son at Oxford and having also met him at Hawarden. The visit to Rome threw him much into their society, and he became engaged to Lady Glynne's eldest daughter.

'In 1839,' writes Sir Francis Doyle, 'I attended Mr. Gladstone's wedding at Hawarden as his best man. Catherine Glynne and her sister Mary, both beautiful women, were married on the same day—the first to William Gladstone, the second to Lord Lyttelton. The occasion was a very interesting one from the high character of the two bridegrooms and the warmth of affection shown for the two charming young ladies by all their friends and neighbours in every rank of life. There was a depth and genuineness of sympathy diffused around which, as the French say, spoke for itself without any words.'

During the early part of their married life Mr. and Mrs. Gladstone lived with Sir Thomas Gladstone at 6, Carlton Gardens. Later they lived at 13, Carlton House Terrace, and when Mr. Gladstone was in office occupied an official residence in Downing Street. In 1850, Mr. Gladstone, who had succeeded to his patrimony five years before, bought 11, Carlton House Terrace, which was his London house for twenty years, and he subsequently lived in Harley Street, where on one occasion an angry mob smashed his windows. During the Parliamentary recess Mr. and Mrs. Gladstone divided their time between Fasque, Sir John Gladstone's seat in Kincardineshire, and Hawarden House, which they shared with Mrs. Gladstone's brother, Sir Stephen Glynne, till, on his death, it passed into their sole possession. Mr. Gladstone had a numerous family. His eldest son predeceased him; his second son is known as Herbert Gladstone; another was Henry Gladstone. One of his daughters married the Rev. Mr. Drew.

It is interesting to read what an American writer has to say of Mrs. Gladstone: 'The French have a derisive saying that there are no political women in England, and hence no salons in London. They have no appreciation of that class of Englishwomen, who are far more important and beneficial to society than are the corresponding class in France. But there is a social factor in English politics unattainable by any other nation, and possibly only under just such a form of Government and with such a ruler as Queen Victoria has proved herself to be. She is in a large sense the leader of the woman movement in her country—a movement which is represented in a stricter sense by Mrs. Gladstone, the wife of England's foremost statesman. In this movement are no diplomats or political female deputies; but women who, knowing the practical work that must be done for humanity, are about it in earnest fashion, giving the world fitting examples of their ability and power as women and workers. To better the condition of the people, not to scheme and wire-pull for a party, is the aim of women like Mrs. Gladstone, whose social power is stronger than the strongest political influence that exists.

'She is a noble woman, aside from the fact that her position is so exceptional that her faults would naturally seem trivial, surrounded by the halo of her rank and her husband's fame. As a little child she exhibited the unselfishness which has made her name beloved in England. Her father said of her that she was his most gifted child, and always spoke with subdued pride of the strong character she exhibited in earliest youth. She chose as a schoolgirl the motto, "If you want a thing well done, do it yourself," and has kept it as hers through life. The practical good sense manifested by her when young has been her magic wand through all the passing years. She is now a woman of seventy-six years, and is the same wise-minded, sensible person that she was when she wrote her chosen sentence in her diary fully seventy years ago. The story of her life would read like a beautiful romance, so full has it been of work, domestic, social, and philanthropic, and so overflowing with happiness.

'The variety and interest which have marked Mrs. Gladstone's life would have been lacking to a large extent had she not felt such an overflowing sympathy for the people—for the poor and trouble-burdened, the weary and the faint-hearted. One of her friends was once lamenting to her that she could do nothing for others because she had not means. "Oh yes, you can, my dear: you can do everything; you can love them." "But that would not help the poor or the sick or the dying," was answered. "Yes, it would; it would cheer and bless and comfort; try it and prove my words," said Mrs. Gladstone, and her visitor parted from her in tears, so heartfelt and earnest were her words.

'The story of Mr. Gladstone's public career is in part his wife's; for in all his undertakings she has been a powerful factor. Wherever he has journeyed she has gone: in whatever work he has been engaged she has been at his side, mastering details and keeping pace with him, so that she has been his comrade in all things. Mr. Gladstone at all times, and on every fitting occasion, pays tribute to the mind and heart of his wife, and attributes to her companionship and encouragement the stimulus and the solace without which he could not have undertaken the tasks he has performed. She was his "helpmeet" from their earliest union, and as time passed and their affection for each other grew as a protecting shelter about them, he relied more and more upon her counsels. Always at his side ministering to him and diverting his mind by steady cheerfulness and bright talk, she has made his life an exceptionally joyous one, and she basks in the sunshine of the happiness she has created. For many years, while her children were growing up about her and needing her watchful care, she had manifold duties, but for a long time there has been no divided responsibility, and the accustomed way for both of them has been together, and together in a union so close that it is really that exceptional thing—a soul-marriage. She alone has shared alike in his labours and his recreations, his triumphs and defeats, and, beyond all the incidents of their united lives, her unselfish devotion has been his staff and his support.

'Mr. Gladstone's manners, especially when addressing ladies, are very courtly. There is a fine stateliness, and at the same time an exquisite courtesy, in his address. In his manners, as well as in much else, Mr. Gladstone belongs distinctly to the older school which flourished before the Queen came to the throne, when society still preserved a certain distinctive style, which has suffered much in the rush and tumble of our new democracy.'

Mr. Gladstone's 'Church Principles and Government' appeared in 1840. Macaulay writes to Napier: 'I do not think it would be wise to review it. I observed in it very little that had reference to politics—very little, indeed, that could not consistently be said by a supporter of the voluntary principle. It is, in truth, a theological treatise, and I have no mind to engage in a controversy about the nature of the Sacraments, the operation of Holy Orders, the validity of the Church, and such points of learning, except where they are connected with questions of Government. I have no disposition to split hairs about the spiritual reception of the body and blood of Christ in the Eucharist, or about baptismal regeneration.' However, it was subsequently reviewed in the Edinburgh by Henry Roger, of Spring Hill College, Birmingham, in an article on the Right of Private Judgment. Dr. Arnold writes how he was disappointed with the book. Newman writes: 'It is not open to the objections I feared; it is doctrinaire, and I think self-confident, but it will do good.' Maurice thus criticised it: 'His Aristotelianism is, it strikes me, more deeply fixed in him than before, and on that account I do not see how he can ever enter into the feeling and truths of Rationalism to refute it. His notion of attacking the Evangelicals by saying, Press your opinions to these results, and they become Rationalistic, is ingenious, and thought out, I think, with great skill and an analytical power for which I had not given him credit; but after all, it seems to me, an argument which is better for the courts than for a theological controversy.' At Eton, about this time, he was almost worshipped. When he went there to examine the candidates for the Newcastle Scholarship, one of the candidates wrote: 'I wish you to understand that Mr. Gladstone appeared not to me only but to others as a gentleman wholly unlike other examiners of school people. It was not as a politician we admired him, but as a refined Churchman deep also in political philosophy.'

In 1841 he accepted the office of Vice-President of the Board of Trade under Sir Robert Peel, afterwards becoming President as successor to Lord Ripon. In his address seeking re-election at Newark, he declared that the British farmer might rely upon two points—first, 'that adequate protection would be given to him; secondly, that protection would be given him through the means of the sliding scale.' In 1842 he was engaged in the preparation of the revised tariff, by which duties were either abolished or diminished on some twelve hundred articles. Greville writes in the March of that year that he had already displayed a capacity which made his admission into the Cabinet indispensable. In the course of the next year he became President of the Board of Trade and a member of the Cabinet, and the very first act he had to perform was to give his vote in favour of withdrawing the Bill providing for the education of children in factories, which had been violently opposed by the Dissenters on the plea that it was too favourable to the Established Church. In this connection we have the following curious story: A brusque but wealthy shipowner of Sunderland once entered the London office of Mr. Lindsay on business. 'Noo, is Lindsay in?' inquired the northern diamond in the rough. 'Sir!' exclaimed the clerk to whom the inquiry was addressed. 'Well, then, is Mr. Lindsay in, seest thou?' 'He will be in shortly,' said the clerk. 'Will you wait?' The Sunderland shipowner intimated that he would, and was ushered into an adjacent room, where a person was busily employed copying some statistics. Our Sunderland friend paced the room several times, and presently, walking to the table where the other occupant of the room was seated, took careful note of the writer's doings. The copier looked up inquiringly, when the northerner said: 'Thou writest a bonny hand, thou dost.' 'I am glad you think so,' was the reply. 'Ah! thou dost—thou maks thy figures well; thou'rt just the chap I want.' 'Indeed,' said the Londoner. 'Yes, indeed,' said Sunderland. 'I'm a man of few words. Noo, if thou'lt coom o'er to canny auld Sunderland, thou seest, I'll gie thee a hoondred and twenty pund a year, and that's a plum thou doesn't meet with every day in thy life, I reckon—noo then.' The Londoner thanked the admirer of his penmanship most gratefully, and intimated that he would like to consult Mr. Lindsay upon the subject. 'Ah, that's reet!' And in walked Mr. Lindsay, who cordially greeted his Sunderland friend, after which the gentleman at the desk gravely rose and informed Mr. Lindsay of the handsome appointment which had been offered him in the Sunderland shipowner's office. 'Very well,' said Mr. Lindsay, 'I should be sorry to stand in your way; a hundred and twenty pound is more than I can afford to pay you in the department in which you are at present placed. You will find my friend a good and kind master, and, under the circumstances, I think the sooner you know each other the better. Allow me, therefore, to introduce to you the Right Hon. W. Gladstone.' Mr. Gladstone had been engaged in making a note of some shipping returns for his budget. The shipowner was, of course, a little taken aback, but he soon recovered his self-possession, and enjoyed the joke as much as Mr. Gladstone did. Very soon Sir Robert Peel proposed to establish non-sectarian colleges in Ireland, and to increase the grant to Maynooth. This led to Mr. Gladstone's resignation in 1845, but not before he had completed a second revised tariff, carrying on still further the work of commercial reform. In the explanation which he gave for his resignation he was understood to say that the measure with regard to Maynooth was a departure from the principles he had contended for in his books.

Everyone was amazed, and the party he had left was very angry. Greville writes: 'Gladstone's explanation was ludicrous. Everybody said that he had only succeeded in showing that his explanation was quite uncalled for.' It is perfectly clear that no one was able to understand the explanation. In a letter to Mr. W. E. Forster, Cobden wrote: 'Gladstone's speeches have the effect on my mind of a beautiful strain of music; I can rarely remember any clear unqualified expression of opinion on any subject outside his political, economical and financial statements. I remember on the occasion when he left Sir Robert Peel's Government on the Maynooth question, and when the House sat in unusual numbers to hear his explanation, I sat beside Villiers and Ricardo for an hour listening with real pleasure to his beautiful rhetorical involutions and evolutions, and at the close turning round to one of my neighbours and exclaiming, "What a marvellous talent is this! Here have I been listening with pleasure for an hour to his explanation, and I know no more why he left the Government than when he commenced."'

A little prior to this speech Mr. Gladstone had secured a follower in the person of Mr. Stafford Northcote, afterwards Lord Iddesleigh, as private secretary. 'From what I know of Mr. Gladstone's character,' writes Mr. Northcote to his father, 'there is no single statesman of the present day to whom I would more gladly attach myself; and I should think, from the talent he has shown for business since he came into office, there is no one more likely to retain his place unless any revolution takes place.' To another friend, Mr. Northcote, on his acceptance of the office, writes: 'With any other man than Gladstone I might have hesitated longer. But he is one whom I respect beyond measure; he stands almost alone as the representative of principles with which I cordially agree; and as a man of business, and one who, humanly speaking, is sure to rise, he is pre-eminent.' A little later Mr. Northcote writes to a lady: 'I look upon him'

(Gladstone) 'as the representative of the party scarcely developed as yet, though secretly forming, which will stand by all that is dear and sacred, in my estimation, in the struggle which will come ere very long between good and evil, order and disorder, the Church and the world; and I see a very small band collecting around him, and ready to fight manfully under his leading.'

In a letter to a friend, Mr. Gladstone thus explains his retirement from office: 'My whole purpose was to place myself in a position in which I should be free to consider my course without being liable to any just suspicion on the ground of personal interest. It is not profane if I say, "With a great price obtained I this freedom." The political association in which I stood was to me, at the time, the Alpha and Omega of public life. The Government of Sir Robert Peel was believed to be of immovable strength. My place, as President of the Board of Trade, was at the very kernel of its most interesting operations . . . I felt myself open to the charge of being opinionated and wanting in deference to really great authorities, and I could not but see that I should be evidently regarded as fastidious and fanciful, fitter for a dreamer, or possibly a schoolman, than for the active purposes of public life in a busy and moving age.'

While at the Board of Trade Mr. Gladstone found time to devote himself as ardently as ever to ecclesiastical subjects. He was one of the party supremely interested in the establishment of an Anglican Bishop at Jerusalem. Lord Shaftesbury describes how, in connection with the event at a dinner given by Baron Bunsen, 'he' (Gladstone) 'stripped himself of a part of his Puseyite garment, and spoke like a pious man.' Bunsen, writing of Gladstone's speech, says: 'Never was heard a more exquisite speech: it flowed like a gentle and translucent stream. . . . We drove back to town in the clearest starlight, Gladstone continuing, with unabated animation, to pour forth his harmonious thoughts in melodious tones.'

In 1845 Mr. Gladstone contemplated a visit to Ireland. 'Ireland,' he writes to an Oxford friend, 'is likely to find this country and Parliament so much occupation for years to come that I feel rather oppressively an obligation to try and see it with my own eyes, instead of using those of other people, according to the limited measure of my means.' The visit, however, was not paid. He went to see Dr. Dollinger at Munich instead.

In the winter Mr. Gladstone, while out shooting, met with an accident that necessitated the amputation of the first finger of his left hand.

It must not be forgotten that early in his official career Mr. Gladstone was Under-Secretary for the Colonies under Lord Aberdeen. Henry Taylor, who was then one of the permanent officials, writes: 'I rather like Gladstone, but he is said to have more of the devil in him than appears, in a virtuous way—that is, only self-willed. He may be all the more useful here for that. His amiable looks and manners deluded Sir James Stephen, who said that for success in public life he wanted pugnacity.' By the time he quitted office, Taylor owns that they had come to know him better. 'Gladstone left with us a paper on negro education, which confirmed me in the impression that he is a very considerable man—by far the most so of any man I have seen among our rising statesmen. He has, together with his abilities, great strength of character and excellent disposition.' In a letter to his friend Hudson Gurney, Lord Aberdeen, one of the ablest statesmen modern England has known, writes: 'In consequence of the defeat of my Under-Secretary in the county of Forfar, I have been obliged to appoint another. I have chosen a young man whom I did not know, and whom I never saw, but of whose good character and abilities I have often heard. He is the young Gladstone, and I hope he will do well. He has no easy part to play in the House of Commons, but it is a fine opening for a young man of talent and ambition, and places him in the way to the highest distinction. He appears to me so amiable that I am sure, personally, I shall like him.' It is interesting in this connection to note Mr. Gladstone's opinion of Lord Aberdeen. He thus describes the interview: 'I knew Lord Aberdeen only by public rumour. I had heard of his high character, but I had also heard of him as a man of cold manners and close and even haughty reserve. It was dusk when I entered the room, so that I saw his figure rather than his countenance, and I remember well that before I had been three minutes with him all my apprehensions had melted away like snow in the sun, and I came away from that interview conscious indeed—as who could not fail to be conscious—of his dignity, but of a dignity so tempered by a peculiar purity and gentleness, and so associated with impressions of his kindness and even friendship, that I believe I thought more about the wonder at that time of his being so misunderstood by the outer world than about the new duties and responsibilities of my new office.' Ministers were beaten by Lord John Russell, who carried a resolution in favour of applying the surplus revenues of the Irish Church to general education, and Mr. Gladstone retired to private life, working hard at his chambers in the Albany, studying mainly Homer and Dante and St. Augustine. He went freely into society, though refusing to attend Mr. Monckton Milnes' Sunday evening parties. He was a frequent attendant at St. James's, Piccadilly, and at All Saints', Margaret Street—all the while speaking when occasion required in Parliament and working hard on Committees.

CHAPTER IV. M.P. FOR OXFORD UNIVERSITY.

In 1845 the Whigs, failing to form a Cabinet, resigned, and Sir Robert Peel was again in office to carry the abolition of the Corn Laws. After resigning office, Mr. Gladstone published a pamphlet on 'Recent Commercial Legislation,' the tendency of which was in favour of the conclusion that all materials of industry should, as far as possible, be set free from Custom duties. When Lord Stanley refused to accompany his chief in the achievement of Free Trade in corn, Mr. Gladstone became, in his place, Secretary of State for the Colonies. But the Duke of Newcastle would not allow Mr. Gladstone his seat for Newark—he had turned his own son, Lord Lincoln, out of the representation of Nottingham for a similar reason—and Mr. Gladstone was out of Parliament when the question of Free Trade was being fought and won. Early in 1847 it was announced that there would be a vacancy in the representation of Oxford, and Mr. Gladstone was selected for the vacant seat. It was known to all that to represent Oxford University was Mr. Gladstone's desire, as it had been that of Canning. In May, 1847, a meeting was held in Oxford in favour of Mr. Gladstone's candidature. The canvassing went on with more than the usual excitement in a University constituency. There was an electioneering Gladstonian rhyme worth preserving. The anti-Gladstonians had difficulty in finding a candidate.

The question for the electors was, as Mr. Gladstone put it, 'Whether political Oxford shall get shifted out of her palæozoic position into one more suited to her position and work as they now stand.' On August 2 Mr. Gladstone writes that he heard, not without excitement, the horse's hoofs of the messenger bearing the news of the poll. He was elected by a majority of 173 over Mr. Round, the senior member, Sir Robert Inglis, being some 700 votes in advance of him. Mr. Hope Scott has left it on record that Mrs. Gladstone was a copious worker on her husband's behalf. Sir Robert Peel went down to vote for his colleague. The venerable Dr. Routh, then nearly ninety-two years old, left his seclusion at Magdalen College to vote for him. The feeling of Mr. Gladstone's supporters may be summed up in a letter written by Dr. Moberly, afterwards Bishop of Gloucester, to a doubtful voter:

'For my own part, I certainly disapprove of Mr. Gladstone's vote on the godless colleges in Ireland, and I am not sure, even though I acknowledge the difficulties of the case, whether I approve of that respecting Maynooth; but I feel that I am not specially called on to reward or punish individual voters as to select the deepest, truest, most attached, most efficient advocate for the Church and Universities in coming, and very probably serious, dangers. I think your correspondence with Gladstone's committee has probably done great good. It is very useful that Gladstone should know that there are those who are not satisfied with some of his past acts; but surely you will not press this hitherto useful course to the extreme result of refraining from voting?'

Mr. Gladstone still continued in politics to uphold Conservative traditions, apart from Free Trade. He opposed marriage with a deceased wife's sister; he deprecated the appointment of a Commission to inquire into the Universities; but he vindicated the policy of admitting Jews to Parliament, and defended the establishment of diplomatic relations with the Court of Rome. He supported the alteration of the Parliamentary oath, but was opposed to an abstract attack on Church rates. One domestic sorrow befell him about this time, the death of a little daughter, Catherine, between four and five years old. Another difficulty which gave him much trouble was on an affair which agitated all England at one time, and was known as the Gorham case. Mr. Gorham was an Evangelical clergyman, and the Bishop of Exeter refused to institute on the ground that his views on baptism were not sound; but in March, 1850, the Judicial Committee of the Privy Council held that his teaching was not such as to debar him from preferment in the Church of England. In a letter addressed to the Bishop of London (Bloomfield), entitled 'The Royal Supremacy viewed in the Light of Reason, History, and Common-sense,' Mr. Gladstone contended that the Royal Supremacy was not inconsistent with the spiritual life and inherent jurisdiction of the Church, and that the recent establishment of the Privy Council as a final court of appeal in religious causes was an injurious, and even dangerous, departure from the Reformation settlement. The Bishops, he held, when 'acting jointly, publicly, solemnly, responsibly, are the best and most natural organs of the judicial office of the Church in matters of heresy, and, according to reason, history, and the Constitution in that subject-matter, the fittest and safest counsellors of the Crown.' To that controversy it is due to a great extent that Mr. Hope Scott and Dr. Manning went over to the Church of Rome—the two men on whom in Church matters Mr. Gladstone principally relied. The blow was severe. 'I felt,' said Mr. Gladstone, 'as if I had lost my two eyes.'

In this year Mr. Gladstone was very much depressed. Sir Stafford Northcote writes: 'He (Gladstone) was out of spirits himself about public matters, and did not paint Parliamentary life in rose colour. . . . He is distressed at the position Peel has taken up, and at the want of sympathy between those who had acted for so many years cordially together, and he looks forward to serious Church troubles, which he thinks might possibly drive him out of Parliament.' An idea which, had it been carried out, would have deprived the world of Mr. Gladstone's greatest triumphs, political and oratorical. In that year came up the Don Pacifico affair, and Lord Palmerston's triumph by means of the Romanus civis sum dictum, against which Mr. Gladstone thundered. It was, as Lord Palmerston admitted, a first-rate performance, appealing to the law of Nature and of God, and deprecating the vain conception that we, forsooth, have a mission to be the censors of vice and folly, of abuse and imperfection, among the other countries of the world, a doctrine which Mr. Gladstone subsequently seemed altogether to have departed from.

On the lamented death of Sir Robert Peel, Mr. Gladstone bore eloquent testimonies to the merits of that great man.

In the following winter Mr. Gladstone was in Naples, taken there by the illness of one of his children, for whom the medical men had recommended a warmer climate, and thence he addressed to the Earl of Aberdeen those letters denouncing the atrocities of the Italian Government which for the first time made Mr. Gladstone popular with the English people.

On his return, he found the country excited to a temporary fury, because the Pope had planned Roman Bishops in English counties. To meet it, Lord John Russell carried an Ecclesiastical Titles Bill, which Mr. Gladstone powerfully attacked, and which some twenty years after he had the pleasure of quietly repealing. But the Bill proved a death-blow to Lord John Russell's hold on office, weakened as it was by Lord Palmerston's retirement, in consequence of his unauthorized recognition of Louis Napoleon's coup d'état. Lord Derby came into office, and there was a General Election.

Mr. Gladstone was sent by Lord Derby as a Lord Commissioner to the Ionian Islands, to carry out needed reforms in that part of the world, Her Majesty Queen Victoria having refused her assent to the petition of the Ionian Parliament for union with Greece. But Mr. Gladstone was to reform the Ionian Parliament, so as to make it resemble as much as possible that of England. When he left, his successor, Sir H. Stocks, wrote: 'Gladstone is regretted by many, respected by all. Nothing could have been better than the firmness, judgment, and temper and talent he has shown. It sometimes staggers me to reflect that I have to succeed him.'

It was about this time that M. Thiers paid England a visit, having left France in consequence of the coup d'état. A dinner was made up for him, at which were present Mr. Gladstone, Bulwer the novelist, Lord Elcho, Lord Herbert of Lea, Mr. Hayward, and others. The conversation was varied and animated. Mr. Hayward writes: 'Thiers had the advantage of language and choice of subject, but the general opinion was that Mr. Gladstone was, if anything, the superior conversationalist of the two.'

When the election of 1852 approached, the opponents of Mr. Gladstone, thinking that his friends might have been alienated by his votes on Jewish disabilities and on the Papal Aggressions Bill, brought forward a third candidate for the University, Dr. Marsham, of Merton, in spite of a declaration signed by 1,276 members; but Mr. Gladstone managed to secure a majority of 350. In the debate in November Mr. Gladstone attacked Mr. Disraeli's Budget, and at the election following the Tories again attacked Mr. Gladstone's seat. The opposition was a curious affair—the result of an obscure intrigue—Lord Crompton being put forward apparently without his consent and against his wish. Then Mr. Percival was suddenly brought forward. Mr. Gladstone, however, on a small poll, had a majority of 87, and his seat was saved for the time. As a rule, a University M.P. is supposed to hold his seat for life.

By this time the Tories had become outrageous against Mr. Gladstone. After the defeat of the Derby Government, some of them gave a dinner to Major Beresford at the Carlton, who had been charged with bribery at the Derby election, and had been acquitted. 'After dinner,' writes Mr. Greville, 'when they got drunk, they went upstairs, and found Mr. Gladstone alone in the drawing-room. Some of them proposed to throw him out of the window. This they did not quite dare do, but contented themselves with giving an insulting message or order to the waiter, and then went away.' But Mr. Gladstone remained a member of the club till 1859. On the Coalition Government being formed under Lord Aberdeen, Mr. Gladstone became Chancellor of the Exchequer. His Budget speech, five hours long, held the House spell-bound. It was devoted mainly to remission of taxation. The deficiency thus created was made up by the application of the legacy duty to real property, by an increase of the duty on spirits, and by an extension of the income-tax at 5d. in the pound to all incomes between £100 and £150. The Irish were indignant at the tax being extended to Ireland. One of the few genuine Irish patriots, Mr. J. O'Neil Daunt, writes: 'One of Mr. Gladstone's arguments is curious from its dishonest ingenuity. He extracts from our poverty a pretext for disarming us. Pitt and Castlereagh promised at the Union that Irish taxation should not be approximated to British until an increased prosperity should enable us to bear the increased burden. The prosperity has not come, but the tax must be got. If, says Gladstone, you have not got wealth to be mulcted, your poverty will answer me quite as well. For the purchasing power of £150 is greater in a poor country than a rich one; whence he argues that, as Ireland is poor, an Irish income of £150 is a fitter subject of taxation than an income of equal amount in England. The peculiar beauty of this argument is, that the poorer a country is, the stronger is the force of argument for taxing it.' Evidently Mr. Gladstone's Budget found more favour in English than in Irish eyes. The income-tax, said Mr. Gladstone, was to expire in 1860. Alas! he did not then foresee the Crimean War. On the contrary, everything seemed to betoken a happy future.

In May, 1853, Mr. Greville records an interview he had with Sir James Graham. 'Graham seemed in excellent spirits about their political state and prospects, all owing to Gladstone and the complete success of the Budget. The long and numerous Cabinets, which were attributed in the Times to disunion, were occupied in minute consideration of the Budget, which was there fully discussed; and Gladstone spoke in the Cabinet one day for three hours, rehearsing his speech in the House of Commons, though not quite at such length. . . . He talked of a future head, as Aberdeen is always quite ready to retire; but it is very difficult to find anyone to succeed him. I suggested Gladstone. He shook his head, and said it would not do. He spoke of the great mistakes Derby had made. Gladstone's object certainly was for a long time to be at the head of the Conservative party in the House of Commons, and to join with Derby, who might, in fact, have had all the Peelites, if he had chosen to ally himself with them instead of Disraeli. The latter had been the cause of the ruin of the party.'

In the same year Bishop Wilberforce wrote: 'Lord Aberdeen is now growing to look upon Gladstone as his successor, and so told Gladstone the other day.'

A little while after we find Lord Aberdeen saying: 'Gladstone intends to be Prime Minister. He has great qualifications, but some serious defects. The chief is that when he has convinced himself, perhaps, by abstract reasoning of some view, he thinks that everyone ought at once to see as he does, and can make no allowance for difference of opinion. Gladstone must thoroughly recover his popularity. The Queen has quite got over her feeling against him, and likes him much. . . . I have told Gladstone that when he is Prime Minister I will have a seat in his Cabinet, if he desires it, without an office.'

CHAPTER V. MR. GLADSTONE'S ECCLESIASTICAL OPINIONS.

In April, 1856, Mr. Greville writes of a conversation he had with Graham: 'He began talking over the state of affairs generally. He says there is not one man in the House of Commons who has ten followers—neither Gladstone, nor Disraeli, nor Palmerston . . . that Gladstone is certainly the ablest man there. His religious opinions, in which he is zealous and sincere, enter so largely into his political conduct as to form a very serious obstacle to his success, for they are abhorrent to the majority of this Protestant country, and (I was surprised to hear him say) Graham thinks approach very nearly to Rome.'

While absorbed in politics, or literature, or society, Mr. Gladstone never forgot to do his duty to the best of his ability as a loyal son of the Church of England. In 1842 there was a fight at Oxford University on the choice of a Professor of Poetry for the University. One candidate was dear to the High Church party, the other to the Low, or Evangelical, of which Lord Ashley was the head. Mr. Gladstone wrote to Lord Sandon, urging him to entreat Lord Ashley to avoid, for the Church's sake, the scandal of a contest. But Lord Ashley was on the winning side, and his candidate was returned at the head of the poll.

In 1843, in the debates on the Dissenters' Chapel Bill, Lord Ashley writes: 'That inexplicable Mr. Gladstone contended that all Dissent was semi-Arian, and that a vast proportion of the founders were, in fact, Unitarians.' When, in 1845, Mr. Ward was condemned at Oxford for his book, 'The Ideal of a Christian Church,' Mr. Gladstone was one of the non-placets. In a letter to his friend Bishop Wilberforce in 1844, Mr. Gladstone writes: 'I rejoice to see that you are on the whole hopeful. For my part, I heartily go along with you. The fabric consolidates itself more and more, even while the earthquake rocks it; for, with a thousand drawbacks and deductions, love grows warmer and larger, truth firmer among us. It makes the mind sad to speculate on the question how much better all might have been, but our mourning should be turned into joy and thankfulness while we think also how much worse it might have been. It seems to me to be written for our learning and use: "He will be very gracious unto thee at the voice of thy cry; when He shall hear it, He will answer thee. And though the Lord give you the bread of adversity and the water of affliction, yet shall not thy teachers be removed into a corner any more, but thine eyes shall see thy teachers: and thine ears shall hear a word behind thee, saying, This is the way, walk ye in it."'

About this time Mr. Gladstone seems to have taken a leading part in the establishment of the High Church College, Glenalmond, instituted for the purpose of turning Presbyterian Scotland from the errors of its ways. At that time Mr. Gladstone was still in bondage. He argued for the maintenance of the Established Church in Ireland. Mr. Gladstone had not advanced beyond his party, and belonged to the school immortalized in 'Tom Jones.' 'When I mention religion,' says the Rev. Mr. Thwackum, 'I mean the Christian religion, and not only the Christian religion, but the Protestant religion, and not only the Protestant religion, but the Church of England.'

In opening the Liverpool Collegiate Institution, he pleaded earnestly for Christian teaching. 'If you could erect a system,' he said, 'which presents to man all branches of knowledge save the one that is essential, you would only be building up a tower of Babel, which, when you had completed it, would be the more signal in its fall, and which would bury those who had raised it in its ruins. We believe that if you can take a human being in his youth, and make him an accomplished man in natural philosophy, in mathematics, or in the knowledge necessary for the profession of a merchant, a lawyer, or a physician; that if in any or all of these endowments you could form his mind—yes, if you could endow him with the power and science of a Newton, and so send him forth, and if you had concealed from him—or, rather, had not given him—a knowledge and love of the Christian faith, he would go forth into the world, able, indeed, with reference to those purposes of science, successful with the accumulation of wealth for the multiplication of more, but poor and miserable and blind and naked with reference to everything that constitutes the true and sovereign purpose of our existence—nay, worse with respect to the sovereign purpose than if he had still remained in the ignorance which we all commiserate, and which it is the object of this institute to assist in removing.'

But Mr. Gladstone was moving. When Lord John Russell brought in a Bill to admit Jews to Parliament, Mr. Gladstone supported it, though at one time against it.

In 1850 Mr. Gladstone wrote a letter to Bishop Hampden, which threw a good deal of light on his mental working. He wrote: 'Your lordship will probably be surprised at receiving a letter from me. The simple purport of it is to discharge a debt of the smallest possible importance to you, yet due, I think, from me, by expressing the regret with which I now look back on my concurrence in a vote of the University of Oxford in the year 1836, condemnatory of some of your lordship's publications. I did not take actual part in the vote, but, upon reference to a journal kept at the time, I find that my absence was owing to an accident. For a good many years past I have found myself ill able to master books of an abstract character, and I am far from presuming at this time to form a judgment on the merits of any proposition then at issue. I have learned, indeed, that many things which in the forward precipitancy of my youth I should have condemned are either in reality sound or lie within the just bounds of such discussion as justly befits a University. But that which (after a delay due, I think, to the cares and pressing occupations of political life) brought back to my mind the injustice of which I had unconsciously been guilty in 1836 was my being called upon as a member of the Council of King's College in London to concur in a measure similar in principle with respect to Mr. Maurice—that is to say, in a condemnation couched in general terms, which really did not declare the point of imputed guilt, and against which perfect innocence could have no defence. I resisted to the best of my power, though ineffectually, the grievous wrong done to Mr. Maurice, and urged that the charges should be made distinct, that all the best means of investigation should be brought to bear on them, ample opportunity given for defence, and a reference then made, if needful, to the Bishop in his proper capacity of layman, as the Council were inexorable. It was only, as I have said, after mature reflection that I came to perceive the bearing of the case on that of 1836, and to find that by my resistance I had condemned myself. I then lamented that on that occasion, now so remote, I had not felt and acted in a different manner. I beg your lordship to accept this, the expression of my cordial regret.' Dr. Hampden had published certain lectures which afterwards were strongly objected to by the Tractarian party, whose triumph led to a good deal of bitterness, hard to understand now.

Again, in March, 1865, when Mr. Dillwyn moved that 'the present position of the Irish Church is unsatisfactory, and calls for the earliest attention of Her Majesty's Government,' Mr. Gladstone replied that they were not prepared to deny the abstract truth of the former part of the resolution, while they could not accept the resolution. The Irish Church as she then stood was in a false position. She ministered only to one eighth or one ninth of the community. The debate was adjourned, and not resumed during the remainder of the session; but the speech of the Chancellor of the Exchequer caused great excitement, and Mr. (afterwards Chief Justice) Whiteside promptly denounced it as fatal to the Established Church of Ireland. Sir Stafford Northcote wrote: 'Gladstone made a terrible long stride in his downward progress last night, and denounced the Irish Church in a way that shows how by-and-by he will deal not only with it, but the Church of England, too . . . was evidently annoyed that his colleagues had decided on opposing Dillwyn's motion. He laid down the doctrine that the tithes were national property. . . . It is plain that he must hold that the tithe of Wales, where the Dissenters are in a minority, does not properly belong to the Church; and by-and-by we shall find that he will carry the principle a great deal further. It is sad to see what he is coming to.'

Tory suspicion soon found a vent; an election was at hand, and Mr. Gladstone's seat for Oxford University was in danger. As early as 1861 the question of his retirement had been mooted. In that year he wrote to the Rector of Exeter College: 'I have never forgotten the ties which bind me to my kind and good-natured supporters in the University, and no prospect elsewhere could induce me to quit them, unless I could think that at a juncture like this they might, with every prospect of success, support a candidate who would fill my place to their full and general satisfaction. . . . To quit Oxford under any circumstances would be to me a most sad, even if it ever became a prudent and necessary, measure.'

As a further illustration of Mr. Gladstone's Liberal opinions, and his unfitness for Oxford, I quote from a letter of his to Bishop Wilberforce on Mr. Hadfield's proposal in the House of Commons to abolish the declaration made by Mayors that they would not use their office against the Established Church. 'As I apprehend the matter, no one is obliged to take this declaration at all. I took it myself last year, as Elder Brother of the Trinity House, in which I have no duty whatever to discharge, except, I believe, to appoint an "almsbody" once in five or ten years. As Chancellor of the Exchequer I have not taken it. An annual Act of Indemnity passes with your consent to dispense with it, and all who choose avail themselves of the dispensation. I put it to you that this declaration ought not to be maintained upon the Statute Book. If it is right to require of certain persons that they should declare something on behalf of the Established Church, the law, and not the individual, should define who those persons should be. An established legal præmunire of self-exception is fatal to the law. If you are right in saying (which I have never heard elsewhere) that men wish to escape the declaration in order that they may carry their municipal paraphernalia in state to Dissenting chapels, it is plain that they can do it now, and therefore the declaration cannot be maintained on the ground that it prevents them, for it does not. If I am told that the mere abstract existence of such a declaration, counteracted as it is by the indemnity, deters the flesh and blood of Dissenting Mayors from such a use of the paraphernalia, such a reply appears to me fanciful. In short, if this Bill is not to be supported, it appears to me better to profess thorough-going exclusiveness at once, and to say that nothing shall be yielded except to force, for that is what the whole matter comes to. . . . It is quite obvious that if the consideration of these measures is to be approached in such a frame of mind, we shall be doing in our day simply what Eldon and Inglis did in theirs. I must say that is not my idea of my stewardship.'

Again, he writes to the Bishop: 'The policy of the Church as an establishment to my mind is plain. She should rest on her possessions and her powers, parting with none of them, except for equivalents in another currency, or upon full consideration of pros and cons; but outside of these she should avoid all points of sore contact with Dissenters. Each one of them is a point at which she as a dead mass rubs upon the living flesh, and stirs the hostility of its owner. It is no less due to her own interests to share them than it is to justice as regards the Dissenter to surrender these points—if surrender that is to be called which is so unmixedly to her advantage.'

In 1865 the Oxford University election resulted in the loss by Mr. Gladstone of his seat. The opposition to him was headed by Archdeacon Denison, on account of his conduct on the Education Question. Mr. Gladstone was defeated by Mr. Hardy, but he was defeated by those members of the constituency who had the least interest in education. Nearly all the professors, tutors, and lecturers voted in the minority, but were outnumbered by the country clergy. 'Of course,' writes Bishop Wilberforce to Mr. Gladstone, 'if half of these men had known what I know of your real devotion to our Church, that would have outweighed their hatred to a Government which gave Waldegrave to Carlisle, and Baring to Durham, and the youngest Bishop on the Bench to York, and supported Westbury in denying the faith of our Lord. But they could not be made to understand the truth, and have inflicted on the University and the Church the gross indignity of rejecting the best, noblest, and truest son of each, in order to punish Shaftesbury'—supposed to be Palmerston's Bishop-maker—'and Westbury. You were too great for them.'

Mr. Gladstone's reply was as follows:

'Do not conceal from yourself that my hands are very much weakened. It is only as representing Oxford that a man whose opinions are disliked and suspected could expect or could have a title to be heard. I look upon myself now as a person wholly extraneous on one great class of questions; with respect to legislative and Cabinet measures, I am a unit. I have had too much of personal collision with Westbury to be a fair judge in his case, but in your condemnation of him as respects attacks on Christian doctrines do not forget either what coadjutors he has had or with what pitiful and lamentable indifference not only the Christian public, but so many of the clergy—so many of the warmest religionists—looked on. Do not join with others in praising me because I am not angry, only sorry, and that deeply. . . . There have been two great deaths or transmigrations of spirit in my political career—one very slow, the breaking of ties with my original party; the other very short and sharp, the breaking of my tie with Oxford. There will probably be a third, and no more.'

In a subsequent letter Mr. Gladstone states to the Bishop his fixed determination never to take any step to raise himself 'to a higher level in official life; and this not on grounds of Christian self-denial, which would hardly apply, but on the double ground, first, of my total ignorance of my capacity, bodily or mental; and secondly, perhaps I might say specially, because I am certain that the fact of my taking it would seal my doom in taking it.' The Bishop and Mr. Gladstone seem ever to have been on the most confidential terms.

In a subsequent debate on Church rates Mr. Gladstone, while opposing an abstract resolution on the subject, declared that he felt as strongly as anyone the desirability of settling the question. The evils attending the present system were certainly enormous, and it was a fact that we had deviated from the original intention of the law, which was not to oppose a mere uncompensated burden on anyone, but a burden from which everyone bearing it should receive a benefit, so that while each member of the community was bound to contribute his quota to the Church, every member of the Church was entitled to go to the churchwardens and demand a free place to worship his Maker. The case then was, especially in towns, that the centre and best parts of the church were occupied by pews exclusively for the middle classes, while the labouring classes were jealously excluded from every part of sight and hearing in the churches, and were treated in a manner which it was most painful to reflect upon.

Sir George Lewis predicted that the death of Peel would have the effect upon Gladstone of removing a weight from a spring, and the worthy Baronet judged correctly. 'He will come forward more and more, and take more part in discussion. The general opinion is that Gladstone will give up his Free Trade and become leader of the Protectionists.' It was not so; Mr. Gladstone had been a puzzle and wonder to his contemporaries. It puzzled the gigantic intellect of a Brougham to understand, not why Mr. Gladstone gave up office when Sir Robert Peel proposed to increase the grant to Maynooth, but Mr. Gladstone's explanation of his conduct. Mrs. Charlotte Wynne, no superficial observer, wrote: 'Mr. Gladstone has been given two offices to keep him quiet, by giving him too much to do to prevent his troubling his head about the Church; but,' adds the lady, 'I know it will be in vain, for to a speculative mind like his theology is a far more inviting and extensive field than any that is offered by the Board of Trade.' This trait of his character especially came out when he opposed the Ecclesiastical Titles Bill, hurried through Parliament in a panic because the Pope had given English titles to his Bishops in England. Mr. Gladstone ever loved to talk of theology, and in 1870 we find him in Dr. Parker's pulpit in the City Temple describing preachers—especially Dr. Newman, who, with his deep piety and remarkable gifts of mind, he described as an object of great interest, and Dr. Chalmers. Their very idiosyncrasies, Mr. Gladstone argued, were in their favour. In 1870, when Mr. Gladstone went to Mill Hill to address the scholars at the Dissenting Grammar School there, he ended with an appeal to the lads above all things to strive after Christian growth and perfection. Early Mr. Gladstone learned to give up his prejudices against Dissenters. Often has he confessed that they are the most efficient supporters and source of strength. Miss Martineau was a Dissenter, yet he went out of his way to offer her a pension which she declined. To hear Mr.

Gladstone read the lessons, all the country round flocked to Hawarden Church when the owner of the hall was at home. People laughed when Lord Beaconsfield on a memorable occasion declared that he was on the side of the angels. When Mr. Gladstone spoke on religious topics, people listened to him with respect, because they felt that in all his utterances he was sincere. Of his Christian liberality of sentiment we have a further illustration when he and his son went to hear Mr. Spurgeon, the great Baptist preacher. The event is thus recorded; it took place in the beginning of the year 1882: 'On Sunday evening last Mr. Gladstone and his eldest son were present at the service in Mr. Spurgeon's tabernacle, and occupied Mrs. Spurgeon's pew. Both before and after the service these distinguished gentlemen were together in the pastor's vestry. Mr. Gladstone shook hands heartily with the elders and deacons present, and expressed himself highly delighted with the service. The visit was strictly private, and Mr. Gladstone and his son walked back to Downing Street.' Many were the varying comments on the event. In the chief Opposition paper a writer recalled the fact that many years ago Mr. Spurgeon expressed a wish that the Church of England might grow worse in order that she soon might be got rid of. He then argued that if Mr. Gladstone's sympathy with Mr. Spurgeon is what his presence at the Tabernacle would imply, we have a satisfactory explanation of the unsatisfactory character of Mr. Gladstone's ecclesiastical appointments. Mr. Spurgeon is a foe to the Church; Mr. Gladstone goes to hear him, therefore he is a foe of the Church. Mr. Gladstone, being a foe of the Church, appoints as Bishops, Deans and Canons the men who will do the Church most mischief. Of course, the Saturday Review did its best to make Mr. Gladstone ridiculous in connection with the affair. 'Some jealousy may be aroused in rival Bethels by this announcement, which is, we believe, the first of its kind. But it may possibly be that Mr. Gladstone is going to take a course, and that he will distribute the steps of that course equally among the various tabernacles of his stanchest supporters. The battle of the Constitution is to be fought out in the precincts of Ebenezer, and Ebenezer must be accordingly secured. Mr. Gladstone's plan is unquestionably a wise one.' The Saturday Review wanted to know what made Mr. Gladstone shake hands so heartily with the deacons. 'A proceeding somewhat similar to Mr. Perkes's plan for winning an election.' Perhaps it is in one of Mr. Gladstone's letters to Bishop Wilberforce that we get a clear idea of his view of the Church of England. In 1857 he wrote: 'It is neither Disestablishment nor even loss of dogmatic truth which I look upon as the greatest danger before us, but it is the loss of those elementary principles of right and wrong on which Christianity must itself be built. The present position of the Church of England is gradually approximating to the Erastian theory that the business of the Establishment is to teach all sorts of doctrines, and to provide Christian ordinances by way of comfort for all sorts of people, to be used at their own option. It must become, if uncorrected, in lapse of time a thoroughly immoral position. Her case seems to be like that of Cranmer—to be disgraced first and then burned. Now, what I feel is that the constitution of the Church provides the means of bringing controversy to issue; not means that can be brought at all times to bear, but means that are to be effectually, though less determinately, available for preventing the general devastation of doctrine, either by a positive heresy or by that thesis I have named above, worse than any heresy. Considering that the constitution of the Church with respect to doctrine is gradually growing into an offence to the moral sense of mankind, and that the question is, Shall we get, if we can, the means of giving expression to that mind? I confess that I cannot be repelled by fears connected with the state of the Episcopal Bench from saying Yes. Let me have it if I can, for, regarding the Church as a privileged and endowed body, no less than one with spiritual prerogatives, I feel these two things—if the mind of those who rule and of those who compose the Church is deliberately anti-Catholic, I have no right to seek a hiding place within the pale of her possessions by keeping her in a condition of voicelessness in which all are entitled to be there because none are. That is, viewing her with respect to the enjoyment of her temporal advantages, spiritually how can her life be saved by stopping her from the exercise of functions essential to her condition? It may be said she is sick; wait till she is well. My answer is, She is getting more and more sick in regard to her own function of authoritatively declaring the truth; let us see whether her being called upon so to declare it may not be the remedy, or a remedy, at least. I feel certain that the want of combined and responsible ecclesiastical action is one of the main evils, and that the regular duty of such action will tend to check the spirit of individualism and to restore that belief in a Church we have almost lost.'

Of colonial Bishops Mr. Gladstone had a high admiration. In 1876 he wrote: 'It is indeed, I fear, true that a part—not the whole—of our colonial episcopate have sunk below the level established for it five-and-thirty years ago by the Bishops of those days. But how high a level it was! and how it lifted the entire heart of the Church of England!'

Here it is as well to give some further particulars as to Mr. Gladstone's action with regard to Church matters. In 1836 Mr. Gladstone left the Church Pastoral Aid Society, of which he had become one of the vice-presidents, in consequence of an attempt to introduce lay agency. At all times he was ready to guard and vindicate the religious character of his alma mater. On one occasion Lord Palmerston had expressed a reasonable dislike of a system which compelled the undergraduates 'to go from wine to prayers, and from prayers to wine.' Mr. Gladstone, in reply, said he had a better opinion of the undergraduates who had been so lately his companions. He did not believe that even in their most convivial moments they were unfit to enter the house of prayer. Mr. Gladstone was one of a committee which met at the lodgings of Mr. (afterwards Sir Thomas) Acland in Jermyn Street, which led to the formation of Boards of Education for the different dioceses, and to the establishment of training colleges, with the double aim of securing religious education for the middle classes and the collegiate education of the schoolmasters.

Mr. Gladstone's ecclesiastical leanings soon brought him back to Parliamentary life, in connection with Archbishop Tait's Public Worship Regulation Bill. The grounds of his opposition he affirmed in the following resolutions:

'1. That in proceeding to consider the grounds for the Regulation of Public Worship this House cannot do otherwise than take into view the lapse of more than two centuries since the enactment of the present rubrics of the Common Prayer-Book of the Church of England; the multitude of particulars combined in the conduct of Divine service under their provisions; the doubt occasionally attaching to their interpretation, and the number of points they are thought to have left undecided; the diversities of local custom which under these circumstances have long prevailed; and the unreasonableness of proscribing all varieties of opinion and usage among the many thousands of congregations of the Church distributed throughout the land.

'2. That this House is therefore reluctant to place in the hands of any single Bishop—on the motion of one or more persons, however defined—greatly increased facilities towards procuring an absolute ruling of many points hitherto left open and reasonably allowing of diversity, and thereby enforcing the establishment of an inflexible rule of uniformity throughout the land, to the prejudice in matters indifferent of the liberty now practically existing.

'3. That the House willingly acknowledges the great and exemplary devotion of the clergy in general to their sacred calling, but is not on that account the less disposed to guard against the indiscretions or thirst for power of other individuals.

'4. That this House is therefore willing to lend its best assistance to any measure recommended by adequate authority, with a view to provide more effectual security against any neglect of, or departure from, strict law which may give evidence of a design to alter, without the consent of the nation, the spirit or the substance of revealed religion.

'5. That in the opinion of this House it is also to be desired that the members of the Church having a legitimate interest in her services should receive ample protection against precipitate and arbitrary changes of established customs by the sole will of the clergyman and against the wishes locally prevalent amongst them, and that such protection does not appear to be afforded by the provisions of the Bill now before the House.

'6. That the House attaches a high value to the concurrence of Her Majesty's Government with the ecclesiastical authorities in the initiative of legislation affecting the Established Church.'

In moving these resolutions, Mr. Gladstone's speech was of the highest interest and importance; 'but never, perhaps, in his long career,' writes the biographer of Archbishop Tait, 'did his eloquence so completely fail to enlist the sympathy even of his own supporters, and the resolutions were withdrawn.' The Bill, opposed by Dr. Pusey on one side and Lord Shaftesbury on the other, was carried in a modified form. Eye-witnesses have described the debate on the second reading: 'The House, jaded with a long and anxious sitting, was eager to divide. A clear voice was heard above the clamour. It was Mr. Hussey Vivian, an old and tried friend of Mr. Gladstone. He rose to warn him not to persist in his amendments; not twenty men on his own side of the House would follow him into the Lobby. Already deft lieutenants, mournful of aspect, had brought slips of paper to their chief, fraught, it seemed, with no good tidings. When the Speaker put the question, there was no challenge for a division. Amid a roar of mixed cheers and laughter, the six resolutions melted away into darkness.'

Sir William Harcourt was one of Mr. Gladstone's principal opponents in the course of the debate. In Committee there was rather an amusing passage of arms between Mr. Gladstone and his old Attorney-General. Sir William espoused the Bill strongly, and implored Mr. Disraeli to come to the rescue. 'We have,' he said, 'a leader of the House who is proud of the House of Commons, and of whom the House of Commons is proud.' A provision had been introduced into the Bill which would have overthrown the Bishops' right of veto on proceedings to be instituted in the New Court. This provision Mr. Gladstone vehemently opposed, and quoted from the canonist Van Espero. Sir William ridiculed the quotations, and accused Mr. Gladstone at the eleventh hour of having come back to wreck the Bill. Two days after he again attacked Mr. Gladstone, and quoted authorities in support of his views. Mr. Gladstone's reply was complete.

At this time Mr. Gladstone was much occupied with his favourite ecclesiastical subjects. In an article on 'Ritual and Ritualism,' contributed to the Contemporary Review, he contended for the lawfulness and expediency of moderate ritual in the services of the Church of England. He returned to Church questions in a second article entitled 'Is the Church of England worth Preserving?'—a question which, of course, he answered in the affirmative. In the course of his remarks he created a perfect storm of indignation on the part of the Roman Catholics. To meet this Mr. Gladstone published a pamphlet called 'The Vatican Decrees in their Bearing on Civil Allegiance.' One hundred and twenty thousand copies of the pamphlet were sold in a few weeks, and the press was filled with replies. Mr. Gladstone returned to the charge in a pamphlet entitled 'Vaticanism,' in which he contended that in theory the Papal Infallibility was inconsistent with the requirements of civil allegiance. In connection with this subject, let it be briefly stated that in 1880, when Mr. Gladstone returned to power, one of the first things to be settled was the Dissenters' Burial Bill, a subject first brought before the House of Commons by Sir Morton Peto in 1861. The Bill was finally piloted through the House of Commons by Mr. Osborne Morgan, Judge Advocate. Perhaps by this time Mr. Gladstone had become tired of ecclesiastical difficulties. In a letter to the Lord Chancellor respecting fresh legislation on the part of the Archbishop of Canterbury, Mr. Gladstone wrote: 'The thing certainly could not be done by the authority of the Cabinet, were the Cabinet disposed to use it, of which at present I can say nothing.'

About this time a church was built at Stroud Green, near Finsbury Park, at a cost of £11,000, £8,000 of which was contributed by the parishioners and their friends. It was an Evangelical or Low church, but when, on the incumbent's retirement, Mr. Gladstone, claiming the presentation on behalf of the Crown, thought fit to appoint as Vicar a clergyman whose antecedents proved him to be commonly known as ritualistic, the parishioners protested. Petitions against Mr. Linklater's appointment, signed by 2,300 petitioners and members of the congregation, were presented to Mr. Gladstone. The following is a quotation from a letter written by the late Vicar: 'There is a very widespread anxiety through the congregation that the church which their money has built should not pass into the hands of one who does not hold the same Evangelical views, or favour the same simple ritual to which they have been accustomed.' The Bishop also appealed and remonstrated; all was in vain. On August 23, 1885, Mr. Linklater was inducted to the charge of the parish. A majority of the seat-holders at once relinquished their seats; others, we are told, have since followed their example, and some who remained in hope of better things are obliged to acknowledge that their hopes are disappointed. The services most prized by the congregation have been discontinued, and other services introduced which are believed to be unscriptural, contrary to the laws ecclesiastical, and opposed to the plain directions of the Book of Common

Prayer.

CHAPTER VI. MR. GLADSTONE AND THE DIVORCE BILL.

In 1857 there occurred a memorable passage of arms between Mr. Gladstone and Sir Richard Bethell—afterwards Lord Westbury—on the subject of divorce. More than one Commission had reported in favour of establishing a separate court, so that the dissolution of marriage might be effected by judicial separation instead of a special Act of Parliament. By this change the expense incident to the existing procedure would be materially reduced, and the remedy which lay within the reach of the wealthy would be extended to the poor. As the law stood, the privilege of obtaining a relief from the marriage tie depended on a mere property qualification. If a man had £1,000 to spend, he might rid himself of an unfaithful wife; if not, he must remain her husband.

The absurdity of the law was well put by Mr. Justice Maule. A hawker who had been convicted of bigamy urged in extenuation that his wife had been unfaithful to him and deserted him, and that was why he had to take a second wife. In passing sentence, the judge, addressing the prisoner, said: 'I will tell you what you ought to have done under the circumstances, and if you say you did not know, I must tell you that the law conclusively presumes you did. You should have instructed your attorney to bring an action against the seducer of your wife for damages; that would have cost you about £100. Having succeeded thus far, you should have employed a proctor, and instituted a suit in the Ecclesiastical Court for a divorce a mensâ et thoro; that would have cost you £200 or £300 more. When you had obtained a divorce a mensâ et thoro, you had only to obtain a private Act for a divorce a vinculo matrimonii. The Bill might possibly have been opposed in all its stages in both Houses of Parliament, and altogether these proceedings would have cost you £1,000. You will probably tell me that you never had a tenth of that sum, but that makes no difference. Sitting here as an English judge, it is my duty to tell you that this is not a country in which there is one law for the rich and another for the poor. You will be imprisoned for one day.'

The long-postponed Bill was introduced into the Lords, where it passed after unflagging opposition from Bishop Wilberforce. July 24 was the date fixed for its second reading in the House of Commons, but no sooner had the Attorney-General (Bethell) risen to explain the Bill than Mr. Henley interposed with a motion that it be read again in a month. He was supported in this unusual proceeding in a speech of great length and energy by Mr. Gladstone. The motion was negatived by a large majority. On July 30 the Attorney-General made his proposed statement. In the course of his speech he pointedly alluded to Mr. Gladstone as a great master of eloquence and subtle reasoning. 'If that right hon. gentleman had lived—thank Heaven he had not—in the Middle Ages, when invention was racked to find terms of eulogium for the subtilissimi doctores, how great would have been his reputation!' The case against the Bill was presented with the most telling force by Mr. Gladstone. He began by urging the strong feeling against the Bill, and the great danger of precipitancy on legislating in such a House under Government pressure. The Bill undertook to deal not only with the civil consequences and responsibilities of marriage, but also to determine religious obligations and to cancel the most solemn vows; while, though not invested with any theological authority, it set itself up as a square and measure of the consciences of men. 'I must confess,' continued Mr. Gladstone, 'that there is no legend, there is no fiction, there is no speculation, however wild, that I should not deem it rational to admit into my mind rather than allow what I conceive to be one of the most degrading doctrines that can be propounded to civilized men—namely, that the Legislature has power to absolve a man from spiritual vows taken before God.' Mr. Gladstone met the assertion that the Bill made no change in the law, but merely reduced to legislative form what had long had legislative effect, by a direct negative. The Bill carried divorce to the door of all men of all classes, and was therefore to all intents as completely novel as if it had no Parliamentary precedent. Entering upon the theological arguments under protest, as a discussion which could not properly be conducted in a popular assembly, he adduced much historical testimony, particularly that of the Primitive Christian Church, to refute the propositions of the Attorney-General as to the solubility of marriage. Coming down to the Reformation, Mr. Gladstone forcibly summarized Sir Richard Bethell's argument, turning aside for a moment to interpolate an amusing personal reference:

'While I am mentioning my honourable and learned friend, it would be ungrateful in me not to take notice of the undeservedly kind language in which he thanked Heaven that I had not lived and died in the Middle Ages. My hon. and learned friend complimented me on the subtlety of my understanding, and it is a compliment of which I feel the more the force since it comes from a gentleman who possesses such a plain, straightforward, John-Bull-like character of mind— rusticus abnormis sapiens crassaque Minerve. Therefore, and by the force of contrast, I feel the compliment to be ten times more valuable. But I must say, if I am guilty of that subtlety of mind of which he accuses me, I think that there is no one cause in the history of my life to which it can be so properly attributed as to my having been for two or three pleasant years the colleague and co-operator with my hon. and learned friend. And if there was a class of those subtilissimi doctores which was open to competition, and if I were a candidate for admission and heard that my hon. and learned friend was so likewise, I assure him that I would not stand against him on any account whatever.'

Mr. Gladstone's next sally was received with much applause. He contended that the Attorney-General had surpassed himself in liberality, for he gave a ninth beatitude: 'Blessed is the man who trusts the received version'—a doctrine much more in keeping with the Middle Ages and those subtilissimi doctores than with the opinion of an Attorney-General of a Liberal Government in the nineteenth century; that was, Blessed is he who shuts his eyes, and does not attempt to discover historical truth; who discards the aims of legitimate criticism; who, in order to save himself trouble and pass an important Bill without exertion, determines not to make use of the faculties that God has given him, and throws discredit upon scholarship and upon the University of which he is a conspicuous ornament, by refusing to recognise anything but the received version. Referring to the social aspect of the question, Mr. Gladstone with glowing eloquence deplored the change which the Bill would work in the marriage state, as shaking the great idea of the marriage ceremony in the minds of the people, marking the first stage on a road of which they knew nothing, except that it was different from that of their forefathers, and carried them back towards the state in which Christianity found the heathenism of man. In conclusion, he declared that he resisted the measure because it offended his own conscientious feelings; it was a retrograde step, pregnant with the most dangerous consequences to their social interests; it was not desired by the people of this country; it contained a proposal harsh and unjust towards the ministers of religion, and involved an insult to religion itself; and, lastly, because it was brought forward at a time when it was impossible to bring the mind of the country and the House to an adequate consideration of its magnitude and importance. Although he might be entirely powerless in arresting its progress, he was determined, as far as it depended upon him, that he would be responsible for no part of the consequences of a measure fraught, as he believed it to be, with danger to the highest interests of religion and the morality of the people. The speech held the House spellbound, and its conclusion was greeted by prolonged cheering. It was felt that all that could be said against the measure had been said. After a forcible reply from Sir Richard Bethell, in which he addressed himself exclusively to the argument of Mr. Gladstone, who had, he said, on that occasion transcended himself, and, like Aaron's rod, swallowed up all the rest of the opponents of the Bill, the second reading was carried by a majority of 111. It was time Mr. Gladstone exerted himself; he had lost ground last session as being unpractical.

In the October of that year Bishop Wilberforce was at Hawarden, and had much talk with Gladstone. He said: 'I greatly feel being turned out of office. I saw great things to do; I longed to do them. I am losing the best years of my life out of my natural service, yet I have never ceased to rejoice that I am not in office with Palmerston. When I have seen the tricks, the shufflings, he daily has recourse to, as to his business, I rejoice not to sit on the Treasury Bench with him.'

Of course, the Divorce Bill intensified his dislike to the Palmerston regime. Never was there a severer fight than that which took place in Committee. Clause by clause, line by line, almost word by word, the progress of the measure was challenged by an acute and determined opposition. One of the most important amendments was made by Lord John Manners, to give jurisdiction to local courts in cases of judicial separation. A still more important amendment was proposed with the object of extending to the wife the same right of divorce as was given to the husband. On this proposal Mr. Gladstone made a telling speech, founding his argument on the equality of the sexes in the highest relations of life. A further amendment in the same direction was attacked with such ardour by Mr. Gladstone, Lord John Manners, and Mr. Henly, that at length the Attorney-General claimed the right, as having official charge of the Bill, to be treated with some consideration, and then he carried the war into the enemy's country so as to bring Mr. Gladstone again to his feet. He complained bitterly of Sir Richard Bethell's charges of inconsistency and insincerity—'charges which,' he said, 'have not only proceeded from his mouth, but gleamed from those eloquent eyes of his which have turned continuously on me for the last ten minutes.' He commented severely on the Attorney-General's statement of his duty with regard to the Bill. It was pushed by him through the House as a Ministerial duty; he received it from the Cabinet, for whom he considered it his duty to hew wood and draw water.

In the course of the discussion of this clause, which occupied ten hours, Mr. Gladstone made upwards of twenty speeches, some of them of considerable length. He was on his legs every three minutes, in a white heat of excitement. Mr. Gladstone is stated to have told Lord Palmerston that the Bill should not be carried till the Greek Calends, and in reply to the question put to him in the lobby by Sir Richard Bethell—'Is it to be peace or war?'—fiercely replied, 'War, Mr. Attorney—war even to the knife.' 'Gladstone,' he wrote to his wife, 'gives a personal character to the debates.' One of Mr. Gladstone's amendments—to the effect that clergymen having conscientious objections to remarrying of divorced persons were to be exempt from any penalty for refusing to solemnize such marriages—which he was unable to move on account of a domestic calamity, was put forward by Sir W. Heathcote and accepted by the Government, and the long and bitter battle came to an end on August 31, when the third reading passed without a division.

Writing as late as 1887, Mr. Gladstone contends that the Divorce Bill was an error. 'My objection,' writes Mr. Gladstone, 'to the Divorce Bill was very greatly sharpened by its introduction of the principle of inequality. But there is behind this the fact that I have no belief whatever in the operation of Parliamentary enactments upon a vow—a case which appears to me wholly different from that of the Coronation Oath. I think it would have been better to attempt civil legislation only, as in the case of the Deceased Wife's Sister Bill. Lord Westbury and I were pitted in conflict by the Divorce Bill; but he was the representative of a prevailing public opinion, as well as of an Administration—I of an opinion which had become isolated and unpopular. I remember hearing with some consolation from Lord Wensleydale that he was against the principle of the Bill.' It is but fair to add that, after the Act had passed, Mr. Gladstone, with the generous frankness which distinguishes all great men, wrote a letter to the Attorney-General, expressing regret for any language he had used during debates on the Bill which might have given pain. Sir Richard used to say during the course of the debates that Mr. Gladstone was the only debater in the House of Commons whose subtlety of intellect and didactic skill made it a pleasure to cross swords with him.

CHAPTER VII. POLITICS AGAIN.

When Parliament met in 1859, an amendment was moved to the Address in a maiden speech from Lord Hartington, which was carried after a three nights' debate, Mr. Gladstone voting with the Government. Lord Derby and his colleagues instantly resigned. A new Government was formed—Lord Palmerston Premier, Lord John Russell leader of the House of Commons, with Mr. Gladstone as Chancellor of the Exchequer. A spirited opposition to Mr. Gladstone's re-election for the University took place. Lord Chandos—afterwards the Duke of Buckingham—came forward as the Conservative candidate. In an address put forward on his behalf by Professor Mansel, it was stated: 'By his acceptance of office Mr. Gladstone must now be considered as having given his adherence to the Liberal party as at present reconstructed, and as approving of the policy of those who overthrew Lord Derby's Government at the late division. By his vote on that division Mr. Gladstone expressed his confidence in the Administration of Lord Derby. By accepting office he now expresses his confidence in the administration of Lord Derby's opponent and successor.' In a letter to Dr. Hawkins, the Provost of Oriel, Mr. Gladstone wrote: 'Various differences of opinion, both on foreign and domestic matters, separated me during great part of the Administration of Lord Palmerston from a body of men with the majority of whom I had acted in perfect harmony under Lord Aberdeen. I promoted the vote of the House of Commons, which in February led to the downfall of that Ministry. Such having been the case, I thought it my clear duty to support, as far as I was able, the Government of Lord Derby. Accordingly, on the various occasions during the existence of the late Parliament when they were seriously threatened with danger of embarrassment, I found myself, like many other independent members, lending them such assistance as was in my power.'

The Oxford election terminated in Mr. Gladstone's triumph over his opponent. It is curious to note how entirely Mr. Gladstone concurred with Lord John Russell. He worked hard in the Cabinet and in Parliament for his lordship's Reform Bill, and regarded with aversion Lord Palmerston's fortifications. In a letter to Her Majesty we read: 'Viscount Palmerston hopes to be able to overcome his objections, but if that should prove impossible, however great the loss to the Government by the retirement of Mr. Gladstone, it would be better to lose Mr. Gladstone than to run the risk of losing Portsmouth or Plymouth.' When his colleague's scruples had been overcome, Lord Palmerston wrote to his Sovereign: 'Mr. Gladstone told Lord Palmerston this evening that he wished it to be understood that, though acquiescing in the step now taken about the fortifications, he kept himself free to take such course as he might think fit upon the subject next year; to which Lord Palmerston consented. That course will probably be the same which Mr. Gladstone took last year—namely, ineffectual opposition and ultimate acquiescence.'

Mr. Gavan Duffy has given us a correct picture of Gladstone as he appeared to him about this time: 'Mr. Gladstone was not yet the official leader of the Peelites, but he was the most noteworthy of them, and attracted close observation. He was habitually grave, it seemed to me, and spoke as if he uttered oracles; yet he left the impression that his speeches were not only improvised, but that the process of adopting a conclusion was not always complete when he rose to speak. But the vigour and grace of his rhetoric put criticism to flight. The House, which relished the persiflage of Palmerston, thought Gladstone too serious, and resented a little, I think, the subdued tone of contemptuous superiority in which he addressed the leader of the House. He was as smooth as silk, but there was manifestly a reserve of vehement and angry passion ready to break out when it was provoked.'

In a book just published by Mr. Hogan we get a glance at Mr. Gladstone as Colonial Secretary. In Queensland a town still bears his name. The town of Gladstone, which is now within the limits of North Queensland, has been somewhat overshadowed by Rockhampton, which owes its existence to the gold fever which, at the time when folk began to talk of 'North Australia,' nobody foresaw. The period, indeed, seems to us now curiously remote, though it is still fresh in the mind of the statesman whose name was bestowed upon the capital of the intended new colony. So much, at least, appears from the prefatory note addressed to the author:

Mr. Hogan deals with the decline and fall of transportation. It had ceased in New South Wales before Mr. Gladstone came into office. It had broken down also in Norfolk Island, and the hideous practice in Van Diemen's Land, known as 'the probation system,' was causing considerable excitement. It was at this time that Lord Stanley conceived the notion of a new penal colony in North Australia, and it fell to his successor, Mr. Gladstone, to give it form and substance. Mr. Hogan does not spare Mr. Gladstone's political errors; he is, on the contrary, rather given to dwelling upon them with an acerbity which is to be regretted. We all know that the venerable statesman, who has now well-nigh outlived the bitterness of party rancour, had in those days much to learn. He was undoubtedly, at one time, of opinion that the right of the mother country to found penal settlements at the Antipodes was incontestable; but this view was then shared by most politicians outside the thoughtful circle of the Philosophical Radicals. It is clear, moreover, that Mr. Gladstone came to the subject of transportation with a sincere conviction that it was possible to convert criminals into good citizens, whose presence on the soil would be, not a curse, but an advantage. There is a remarkable State paper in the shape of a memorandum addressed to Sir Eardley Wilmot, who had been sent out specially to inaugurate the probation system. In this, after commenting with the enthusiasm natural to a young statesman on the practicability of reformation, he goes on to say: 'Considerations yet more sacred enhance the importance of it, for it is impossible to forget in how large a proportion of cases these unhappy people have every claim on our sympathy which the force of temptation, adverse circumstances of life, ignorance and neglected education, can afford to those who have incurred the penalty of the law.'

But our colonists, no doubt, saw in such utterances only a pharisaism which overlooks the fact that this is pre-eminently a sort of charity which should begin at home. Mr. Gladstone, as appears from his despatches, was profoundly dissatisfied with the way in which Sir Eardley Wilmot—who was an old man, with probably an old-fashioned aversion to new ideas—performed, or, rather, did not perform, his duties, and finally dismissed him. Unfortunately, at the same time he addressed him in a private or 'secret' letter, in which he referred to certain rumours that had reached him of irregularities in Sir Eardley's private life, which, as they were subsequently disproved, and Sir Eardley died during the controversy, awakened much sympathy. Mr. Hogan gives great prominence to this old scandal, and there can be no doubt that Sir Eardley was unjustly treated; but it is manifest that it was not the malicious rumours, but the neglect of duty, that was the ground of his dismissal. Mr. Gladstone's complaint is:

'You have under your charge and responsibility many thousand convicts formed into probation parties, or living together at Government depots. It is only with extreme rarity that you advert in your despatches to the moral condition of these men. You have discussed the economical questions connected with their maintenance or their coercion, and you have even entered into argument, though in a manner too little penetrating, upon their offences against the laws. But into the inner world of their mental, moral and spiritual state, either you have not made it a part of your duty to examine, or else—which for the present issue is, I apprehend, conclusive—you have not placed Her Majesty's Government in possession of the results.'

It is curious to note Mr. Gladstone's unpopularity in the Colonies. When Sir Henry Parkes, the New South Wales Premier, visited England, he writes: 'I had a long conversation with Mr. Gladstone, in the course of which I told him that he had been often charged in Australia, both in the newspapers and in speeches, with being indifferent, if not inimical, to the preservation of the connection between the colonies and England. He was visibly surprised at what I told him, and said I was authorized to say that he had never at any time favoured such view, and that I might challenge any person making the charge to produce proof in support of it.' On another occasion Sir Henry Parkes writes: 'We talked for two hours chiefly on Australian topics, and I recollect very vividly his animated inquiry as to whether many of the young men of the country entered the Church.'

The Budget of 1860 was distinguished mainly for two things—the Commercial Treaty with France, initiated by Mr. Cobden, and the Taxes on Knowledge.

In the debate on this subject in 1852, Mr. Gladstone, then in opposition, intimated that, though he should like to see the paper duty repealed when the proper time had come, if books and newspapers were dearer than they ought to be, the blame was not so much with fiscal requirements as with the trades unionism, which wickedly raised the wages of compositors and others to a level far above their deserts. If the working-classes wanted cheap literature, he thought that they had a sufficient remedy in their own hands, as they themselves could cheapen the labour by which the literature was produced (quoted from Fox Bourne's 'History of the Newspaper Press').

In the following year Mr. Gladstone, after the Government had been beaten, as a compromise, proposed to reduce the advertisement duty from one shilling and sixpence to sixpence. But he was again defeated, and the tax, in spite of him, was abolished altogether. The final stage was reached in 1861, when the paper duty was abolished, Mr. Gladstone being Chancellor of the Exchequer, after the Bill had been defeated in the House of Lords. 'It entailed,' wrote Mr. Gladstone in the Nineteenth Century, 'the severest Parliamentary struggle in which I have ever been engaged.' The repeal of the paper duty was the arrival of a new era in literature—of the penny newspaper, of the popular magazine, of cheap reprints of all our great standard authors.

On February 15 Mr. Greville writes: 'When I left London a fortnight ago the world was anxiously expecting Gladstone's speech, in which he was to put the Commercial Treaty and the Budget before the world. His own confidence, and that of most of his colleagues, in his success was unbounded, but many inveighed bitterly against the treaty. Clarendon shook his head, Overstone pronounced against the treaty, the Times thundered against it, and there is little doubt that it was unpopular, and becoming more so every day. Then came Gladstone's unlucky illness, which compelled him to put off his expose, and made it doubtful whether he would not be physically disabled from doing justice to the subject. His doctor says he ought to have taken two months' rest instead of two days. However, at the end of his two days' delay he came forth and, consensus omnium, achieved one of the greatest triumphs that the House of Commons ever witnessed. Everybody, I have heard from home, admits that it was a magnificent display, not to be surpassed in ability of execution, and that he carried the House of Commons with him. I can well believe it, for when I read the report of it next day it carried me along with it likewise.' The only parties not gratified were the Temperance Reformers, who did not like the cheap Gladstone claret which was immediately introduced at the dinner-tables, nor that clause of the new Bill which was to give grocers licenses to sell the cheap wines of France, and which was to make the fortune of the great house of Gilbey.

Lord Russell became a peer, and left Mr. Gladstone to fight the good fight in the House of Commons, about this time. Gladstone and Disraeli were fully recognised as the leaders of their respective parties. In the life of Mr. Richard Redgrave, under the date of 1860, Mr. Redgrave gives a description of Mr. Gladstone's reply to Mr. Disraeli's attack on the French Treaty. A friend who was present told him: 'Mr. Gladstone was in such a state of excitement that everyone dreaded an attack from him; that his punishment of Mr. Disraeli was most ferocious. He was like a Cherokee Indian fighting; he first knocked down his adversary, then he stamped upon him, then he got excited and danced on him; he scalped him, and then took him between his finger and thumb like a miserable insect, and looked at him, and held him up to contempt.'

Mr. Macarthy's judicious criticism may be quoted here.

'It is idle to contend that between Gladstone and Disraeli any love was lost, and that many people thought it was unhandsome on the part of Mr. Gladstone not to attend his great rival's obsequies, and to bury his animosities in the grave. In 1862 Disraeli complained to the Bishop of Oxford that he and others kept the Church as Mr. Gladstone's nest-egg when he became a Whig till it was almost addled. At this time Disraeli wrote: "I wish you could have induced Gladstone to have joined Lord Derby's Government when Lord Ellenborough resigned in 1858. It was not my fault that he did not; I almost went on my knees to him. Had he done so, the Church and everything else would have been in a very different position." In 1867 the Bishop of Oxford writes: "The most wonderful thing is the rise of Disraeli. It is not the mere assertion of talent, as you hear so many say; it seems to me quite beside that. He has been able to teach the House of Commons almost to ignore Gladstone, and at present lords it over him, and, I am told, says that he will hold him down for twenty years." Disraeli, however, did himself no good when, in 1878, he described Mr. Gladstone as a sophistical rhetorician, inebriated with the exuberance of his own verbosity, and gifted with an egotistical imagination that at all times can command an interminable and inconsistent series of arguments to malign his opponents and to glorify himself.'

Disraeli was never happy in statement. When he had to explain a policy, financial or other, he might really be regarded as a very dull speaker. Gladstone was specially brilliant in statement. He could give to an exposition of figures the fascination of a romance or a poem. Mr. Gladstone never could, under any circumstances, be a dull speaker. He was no equal of Disraeli in the gift of sarcasm, and what Disraeli himself called 'flouts and jeers.' But in his reply he swept his antagonist before him with his marvellous eloquence, compounded of reason and passion.

On the breaking out of the American Civil War, Mr. Gladstone was undoubtedly on the side of the South: Jefferson Davis, he said, had made a nation of the South—a speech of which Mr. Gladstone repented a few years after. But it took a long time for the North to forgive or forget his unfortunate speech. Bishop Fraser, writing in 1865, says: 'They have just got hold of about a dozen subscribers to the Confederate Loan, among whom is W. E. Gladstone, down, to my surprise, for £2,000. This, as you might expect, is a topic for excited editorials, and the cry is that the American Government ought to demand his dismissal from the Ministry.'

In time the Americans began to understand Mr. Gladstone better, and to appreciate him and his good feeling towards their country more. Major Pond, the well-known American, for twenty years endeavoured to get the G.O.M.—as he has long been known on both sides of the Atlantic—to cross the Atlantic on a lecturing tour. In 1880 Mr. Gladstone wrote to him: 'I have to acknowledge the receipt of your letter, with all the kindness it expresses and the dazzling prospects which it offers. Unhappily, my reply lies not in vague expressions of hope, but in the burden of seventy years and of engagements and duties beyond my strength, by desertion of which, even for the time needed, I should really be disentitling myself to the goodwill of the American people, which I prize so highly.' Notwithstanding this refusal, Major Pond returned to the attack, and offered the Grand Old Man seven thousand pounds for twenty lectures, which Mr. Gladstone declined. As a gentleman, he was bound to do so. It would have been a sorry sight to have seen the G.O.M. carted all over America as a show on a lecturing tour.

'To Americans,' says Table Talk, 'the venerable ex-leader of the Liberal Party in the British Parliament is not only a great Englishman, but the greatest of all Englishmen, and his demise, which, it is to be hoped, will yet be long postponed, will be regarded as a calamity to all the English-speaking races. It has always been a matter of keen regret throughout the American continent that Mr. Gladstone has never been able to pay a visit to those whom the Grand Old Man described in his memorable article in the North American Review as "kin beyond sea." In July, 1894, a well-organized attempt was made to induce Mr. Gladstone to cross the ocean. A letter of invitation was sent to him, signed by the then Vice-President of the United States, Mr. Adlai Stevenson, by Mr. Chauncey Depew, by Dr. Pepper, Provost of the University of Pennsylvania, by seventy Senators and one hundred Congressmen, by the Governors of a large number of the States, as well as nearly all the members of Mr. Cleveland's Cabinet and of the Supreme Bench at Washington. It was intimated to the aged statesman that the most extraordinary arrangements would be made for his comfort, including the most luxurious (of course, free) transportation for himself, Mrs. Gladstone, and such companions and attendants as he desired; a special service of private cars on all the railways, and the unlimited use of an Atlantic cable during the time of his absence from England. Mr. Gladstone was also promised immunity from "interviewers, party politicians, advertisers, and hand-shakers." Mr. Gladstone's reply covered three pages of large size writing-paper, and was written by himself entirely. At that time, it will be remembered, Mr. Gladstone's eyes were giving him great trouble, and he pathetically wrote: "Undoubtedly your letter supplied the strongest motives for an attempt to brave the impossible. But I regret to say it reaches me at a time when, were I much younger, it could not be open to me to consider this question." At the same time, while unable to accept such a flattering invitation, Mr. Gladstone, in concluding his letter, begged that the American nation would remain assured of "my unalterable interest in your country."'

It was scarcely necessary to write that. In his celebrated article on 'Kith and Kin' Mr. Gladstone had shown how far our American cousins had shot ahead of the old folks at home.

In 1866 Sir Richard Temple wrote of the opening debate: 'Next it was Mr. Gladstone's turn to speak. I had understood privately that he was going to make some announcement that would imply the resignation of the Liberal leadership. He was known to be disappointed at his failure to obtain a majority at the General Election. . . . In fact, however, he said nothing to imply resignation, but, on the contrary, was evidently prepared to oppose the Government and challenge them to propose a measure in favour of Ireland, if they had one. It was in this speech that, alluding to his reserve on the question of Home Rule until the fit moment for action should arrive, he described himself as an old Parliamentary hand. He had long been a coiner of phrases that have become household words in Parliament, and yet this description became famous among us at once.'

Lord Houghton writes in 1866: 'I sat by Gladstone at the Delameres'. He was very much excited, not only about politics, but cattle plague, china, and everything else. It is indeed a contrast to Palmerston's "Ha, ha!" and laissez faire.' Again in 1868 Lord Houghton writes: 'Gladstone is the great triumph, but, as he owns that he has to drive a four-in-hand consisting of English Liberals, English Dissenters, Scotch Presbyterians, and Irish Catholics, he requires all his courage to look his difficulties in the face, and trust to surmount them.'

In 1849 Lord Malmesbury writes: 'Dined with the Cannings, and met Mr. Gladstone and Mr. Phillimore. We were anxious to see the former, as he is a man much spoken of as one who will come to the front. We were disappointed at his appearance, which is that of a Roman Catholic priest; but he is very agreeable.' On another occasion Malmesbury speaks of Gladstone as 'a dark horse.' In 1866 Lady Palmerston tells Lord Malmesbury that his lordship had very serious apprehensions as to Mr. Gladstone's future career, and considered him a very dangerous and reckless politician. About the same time Lord Palmerston said to the Earl of Shaftesbury: 'Gladstone will soon have it all his own way, and when he gets my place we shall have strange doings.' A little later on Lord Malmesbury refers to the zest with which Mr. Gladstone had taken to singing nigger melodies.

Mr. Gladstone in 1865, questioned on the subject of the Irish Church, wrote: 'It would be very difficult for me to subscribe to any interpretation of my speech on the Irish Church like that of your correspondent, which contains so many conditions and bases of a plan for dealing with a question apparently remote and at the same time full of difficulties on every side. My reasons are, I think, plain. First, because the question is remote, and out of all bearing on the practical politics of the day, I think it would be far worse for me than superfluous to determine upon any scheme or bases of a scheme with respect to it. Secondly, because it is difficult, even if I anticipated any likelihood of being called on to deal with it, I should think it right to take no decision beforehand as to the mode of dealing with the difficulties. But my first reason is that which chiefly sways. As far as I know, my speech signifies pretty clearly the broad distinction between the abstract and the practical views of the subject. And I think I have stated strongly my sense of the responsibility attaching to the opening of such a question except in a state of things which gives promise of satisfactorily settling it. . . . In any measure dealing with the Church of Ireland, I think (though I scarcely expect ever to be called on to share in such a measure), the Act of Union must be recognised, and must have important consequences, especially with reference to the position of the hierarchy.'

A little amusement will be created by the following:

Mr. Jerningham, author of 'Reminiscences of an Attaché,' met Mr. Gladstone at Strawberry Hill just after the Liberal defeat on the Reform Bill. Sitting near him at breakfast, Mr. Jerningham asked Mr. Gladstone for his autograph.

'"Certainly," he said; "but you must ask me a question on paper, and I will answer it."

'I was twenty-three years of age—very proud of being in such interesting company at such a time, and therefore most anxious to justify my presence by some clever question.

'I wrote down quickly the following, and, rather pleased with it, gave it to Mr. Gladstone. It ran thus: "What is Mr. Gladstone's opinion of the difference which exists in 1866 between a Liberal and a moderate Conservative?"

'Mr. Gladstone crumpled up the paper, and, apparently much annoyed, said he did not think he could answer such a question.

'I was so concerned by his look of vexation that I went up to one of the ladies and repeated my question to her, so as to gather from her in which way I had offended.

'She nearly screamed—at least, so far as that person could ever utter a sound—and asked how I could ever have been so bold.

'The truth dawned upon me. The moderate Conservatives of 1866 had dissolved a powerful Liberal Ministry, and I had inquired what he thought of them—of the very statesman who had put their moderate principles to the test.'

After this faux pas one is not surprised that Mr. Jerningham rejoiced that a dinner in town obliged him to leave his hosts on that very afternoon. But, after all, the storm soon blew over, and the incident had a pleasant ending. As Mr. Jerningham was on his way to Richmond, whom should he find upon the boat at Twickenham but Mr. Gladstone himself! So ends the tale:

'I very modestly bade good-bye to him without any allusion to my indiscretion of the morning;

but with infinite kindness and charm of manner, he said, "I have not forgotten you," and pulled out of his pocket my original question and his characteristic answer to it:

Count Beust says: 'When I was ambassador in London, Mr. Gladstone, who was then in office, was caricatured with his colleagues in a piece called "The Happy Land," at the Court Theatre. This annoyed the Premier, and the piece was taken off.'

CHAPTER VIII. POLITICS AND THE IRISH CHURCH.

In the General Election for 1865 Mr. Gladstone lost his seat for the University of Oxford. For years it was evident that his advancing views were gradually drifting him from the Oxford constituents, and when an Act was passed to enable country clergymen and non-resident M.A.'s—by means of voting papers—to swamp the real Oxford constituency, Mr. Gladstone's seat was gone, and his opponent, Mr. Hardy, triumphed. The battle was bravely fought, and the blow was severely felt by Mr. Gladstone and his friends. In his farewell address Mr. Gladstone said: 'After an arduous connection of seven years, now I bid you farewell. My earnest purpose to serve you—my many faults and shortcomings—the incidents of the political relationship between myself and the University established in 1847, so often questioned in vain, and now at length finally dissolved—I leave to the judgment of the future. It is an imperative duty, and one alone which induces me to trouble you with these few parting words—the duty of expressing my profound and lasting gratitude for indulgence as generous, and for support as warm and enthusiastic in itself, and as honourable from the character and distinctions of those who have given it, as has, in my belief, ever been given by any constituency to any representative.'

'The salient figure,' writes Sir Richard Temple, 'was the impressive personality of Mr. Gladstone himself, who was quite the figure-head in this Parliament. Naturally he was no longer the handsome man with the beautiful voice who had been wont to charm a listening senate. But still his attitude was noble, picturesque, and when under excitement he was grandly leonine. Advanced age had left its trace on him outwardly, and had impaired his matchless powers of elocution. The once resonant voice often would become husky, and at times almost inaudible, so that his voice rose and fell with a cadence like the wind. But his persuasiveness for many minds remained in its highest degree. His impassioned gesture seemed to be quieter; it could not conceivably have been finer than it was in those days. When excited in speech, he would sweep his arm round like the play of a scimitar, and yet with a movement both graceful and appropriate. His hands, too, were most impressive, and by their motion or action helped him to enforce his arguments. Above all, there was the play of features on the careworn countenance. Evidently he was in the highest sense of the term one of Nature's orators.' The quality of his speeches was not quite what it had once been in all respects. The passion, the glow, the sympathy, the magnetism remained as of yore.

At the Oxford election Dr. Pusey wrote to a friend: 'You are naturally rejoicing over the defeat of Mr. Gladstone, which I mourn. Some of those who concurred in that election or stood aloof will, I fear, mourn hereafter because they were the cause of that rejection. The grounds alleged against Mr. Gladstone bore at the utmost upon the Establishment. The Establishment might perish and the Church might come forth the purer. If the Church were corrupted the Establishment would become a curse in proportion to its influence. As that conflict will thicken, Oxford will, I think, learn to regret her rude severance from one so loyal to the Church, to the faith, and to God.'

Speaking in the Free Trade Hall in Manchester during the South Lancashire election, Mr.

Gladstone said: 'After an anxious struggle of eighteen years, during which the unbounded devotion and indulgence of my friends have maintained me in the arduous position of representative of the University of Oxford, I have been driven from that position; but do not let me come among you under false colours or with a false pretence. I have loved the University of Oxford with a deep and passionate love, and as long as I live that attachment will continue. If my affection is of the smallest advantage to that great, that noble, that ancient institution, that advantage, such as it is—and it is most insignificant—that attachment Oxford will possess as long as I breathe. But don't mistake the issue which has been raised. The University has at length, after eighteen years of self-denial, been drawn by what I might call the overweening exercise of power into the vortex of mere party politics. Well, you will readily understand why, as long as I had a hope that the zeal and kindness of my friends might keep me in my place, it was not possible for me to abandon them. Could they have returned me by but a majority of one, painful as it is to a man at my time of life, and feeling the weight of public cares, to be incessantly struggling for his seat, nothing could have induced me to quit the University to which I had so long devoted my best care and attachment. But by no act of mine I am free to come among you. And having thus been set free, I need hardly tell you that it is with joy, with thankfulness and enthusiasm that I now, at the eleventh hour, make my appeal to the heart and mind of South Lancashire, and ask you to pronounce upon that appeal.'

Mr. Gladstone then described what had been done by himself and party, commencing with the emancipation of the Roman Catholics, dwelling on the reformation of the Poor Law, the reformation of the tariffs, the abolition of the Corn Laws, the abolition of the Navigation Laws, the conclusion of the French Treaty, the removal of laws which have relieved Dissenters from stigma and almost ignominy, adding: 'I can truly say that there is no period of my life during which my conscience is so clear, and renders me so good an answer, as those years in which I have co-operated in the promotion of Liberal measures. Because they are Liberal they are the true measures, and indicate the true policy by which the country is made strong and its institutions preserved.'

In a speech delivered the same evening at the amphitheatre at Liverpool, Mr. Gladstone continued: 'I am, if possible, more firmly attached to the institutions of my country than when a boy I wandered among the sand-hills of Seaforth. But experience has brought its lessons. I have learned that there is wisdom in a policy of trust, and folly in a policy of mistrust. I have observed the effect which has been produced by Liberal legislation; and if we are told that the policy of the country is in the best and broadest sense Conservative, honesty compels me to admit that that result has been brought about by Liberal legislation.'

About this time the Duke of Newcastle died, leaving Mr. Gladstone a trustee of his son's estate. 'In this capacity,' writes Mr. G. W. E. Russell, 'the Chancellor of the Exchequer applied himself with characteristic thoroughness to the duties pertaining to the management of a rural property, and acquired in the superintendence of the woodlands of Chester that practical knowledge of woodcraft which has since afforded him such constant interest and occupation.'

The new Parliament was opened on February 6, 1866, the Queen appearing at the ceremony for the first time since her widowhood. In offering his services to Earl Russell, after the death of Palmerston, Mr. Gladstone wrote: 'I am sore with conflicts about the public expenditure, which I feel that other men would have escaped, or conducted more gently and less fretfully. I am quite willing to retire.'

As one of the Ministers who engaged in the Crimean War, Mr. Gladstone had to leave office, Lord Derby being unable to form a Ministry, as Mr. Gladstone and the Peelites would not join him. Lord Palmerston became Premier, and Mr. Gladstone returned to office as Chancellor of the Exchequer, but resigned three weeks afterwards, on the ground that the Government assented to Mr. Roebuck's motion for a committee to inquire into the conduct of the war. Twenty years after Mr. Gladstone contended: 'The design of the Crimean War was in its groundwork the vindication of European law against an unprovoked aggression. It sought, therefore, to maintain intact the condition of the menaced party against the aggressor; or, in other words, to defend against Russia the integrity and independence of the Ottoman Empire.' This resignation took place in February, 1855, and Mr. Gladstone's position in consequence became very isolated. According to his subsequent statement, he was driven from office. His sympathies, he owns, were with the Conservatives, his opinions with the Liberals.

The Bishop of Oxford writes of Gladstone as in the highest sense of the term 'Liberal'— 'detested by the aristocracy for his succession duty, the most truly Conservative measure passed in my recollection.' Yet Mr. Gladstone was still as eager as ever in Church matters. Archdeacon Denison had been prosecuted for teaching the doctrine of the Real Presence, and was condemned by Dr. Lushington, acting as assessor to Archbishop Sumner. Gladstone wrote: 'Whatever comes of it, two things are pretty clear: The first, that not only with the executive authorities, but in the sacred halls of justice, there are now two measures, and not one, in use—the straight one, for those supposed to err in believing too much; and the other for those who believe too little. The second is, that this is another blow to the dogmatic principle in the Established Church, the principle on which, as a Church, it rests, and on which, as an establishment, it seems less and less permitted to rest. No hasty judgment is pardonable in these matters; but for the last ten or twelve years the skies have been darkening for a storm.' Again he writes: 'The stewards of doctrine should, on the general ground of controversy and disturbance, deliver from their pulpits, or as they think fit, to the people the true and substantive doctrine of the Holy Eucharist. This freely done, and without any notice of the Archbishop or Dr. Lushington, I should think far better for the time than any declaration.'

Mr. Gladstone, as leader of the House, introduced a Reform Bill Lord Russell laboured at in the Cabinet, which was not very cordial in its favour, but he was supported by Mr. Gladstone, deciding to deal only with the question of the franchise, and leaving the question of redistribution to a later time. The Bill, which was introduced by Mr. Gladstone on March 12, proposed the reduction of the county franchise from £50 to £14, and of the borough franchise from £10 to £7. Some people seemed to think that Mr. Gladstone did not speak with his accustomed force; but that may be accounted for by the remembrance that he had to speak to a House not very enthusiastic in favour of Parliamentary reform. But the first reading was carried after two nights' debate, and the second reading was fixed for April 12. It was, however, evident that, while the Conservative party were organized, the Liberals on their side were divided and indifferent. They argued with some force that the Government had brought forward only half of its scheme, and that it was impolitic and unstatesmanlike to accept one portion of the scheme without being acquainted with the whole. Lord Grosvenor, though sitting on the Liberal benches, declared that he would meet the second reading by a resolution to that effect; while Mr. Kinglake, the author of 'Eothen,' aiming at the same end, but anxious to secure the maintenance of the Government, announced that he should ask the House of Commons to declare that it was not expedient to go into Committee on the Bill until the House had before it the expected Bill for the redistribution of seats. The House, however, passed the second reading, but by a majority so small that the continuance of the Ministry in power was difficult. The Ministry, however, decided to persevere, and in April introduced three additional measures—a Redistribution Bill for England and Wales, and Reform Bills for Scotland and Ireland. But the condition of affairs did not improve—on the contrary, grew worse; and on June 1 Lord Dunkellin, the eldest son of Lord Clanricarde, carried a motion against the Government, substituting rating for rental as the basis of the borough franchise. The Ministry resigned, and Lord John Russell as a Parliamentary leader disappears from history.

There were people who hinted that Lord John was jealous of Mr. Gladstone's success. Such does not seem to have been the case. In 1853 his lordship wrote to Lady John: 'Gladstone's speech was magnificent. It rejoices me to be a party to so large a plan, and to do with a man who seeks to benefit the country rather than to carry a majority by a concession to fear.' Again, when the question of privilege arose on the action of the Lords with regard to the paper duty, Lord John told the Duke of Bedford that Mr. Gladstone's speech was 'magnificently mad.' In 1867 Mr. Gladstone wrote to Lord John: 'My political relations with you have been late in life. I moved to you, not you to me; and ever since we have been in contact—that is to say, during the last fifteen years—my co-operation with you has been associated all along with feelings of warm attachment and regard. Every motion that moves me further from you is painful to me. . . . If you do not stand without a rival, I, for one, do not know where to look for your superior in the annals of British legislation.' A little later on, when Mr. Gladstone brought forward the motion which sounded the knell of the Tory Government and of the Established Church in Ireland, Lord John presided at an enthusiastic meeting, held in St. James's Hall, London, to support Mr. Gladstone's policy; and when, in December, 1868, Mr. Gladstone formed his first Administration, one of the first persons he wrote to to join him was Lord John. Upon the refusal of the latter, on the plea of age, Mr. Gladstone wrote: 'The snapping of ties is never pleasant, but your resolution is probably a wise one. Perhaps it is selfish of me to think of and mention them, rather than dwell upon those ties which inseparably associate your name with so many great and noble passages in the history of our country.' And again, when Mr. Gladstone had introduced his Irish Land Act, he wrote to Lord John: 'We have had a most anxious time with regard to the Irish Land Bill. Often do I think of a saying of yours more than thirty years back, which struck me ineffaceably at the time. You said the true key to an Irish debate was this: that it was not properly borne in mind that as England is inhabited by Englishmen, and Scotland by Scotchmen, so Ireland is inhabited by Irishmen.'

Let us return to the Reform Bill. It was evident that London was getting excited on the subject. When the Liberals resigned in June, some ten thousand people assembled in Trafalgar Square and passed strong resolutions in favour of Reform. They then marched to Carlton House, singing litanies and hymns in honour of Mr. Gladstone. As he was away, Mrs. Gladstone and her family came out on the balcony to acknowledge the popular tribute. At meetings all over England Mr. Gladstone was hailed as the hero of the people. He had become 'the People's William.' On July 13 Lord Houghton wrote to a friend on the Continent: 'The change of Ministry has passed over very quietly. It was a real collapse, and inevitable by human skill. Gladstone showed a fervour of conviction which has won him the attachment of three hundred men and the horror of the rest of the House of Commons. He will be all the better for a year or two of opposition.' It was in the course of this debate that Mr. Gladstone, replying to Lord R. Montagu's expression that the working classes, if armed with the franchise, would be an invading and destroying army, evoked a ringing cheer when, in a climax of enthusiasm, he asked: 'Are they not our own flesh and blood?'

In the autumn Mr. Gladstone, with his family, spent a short while in Rome, where he had an interview with the Pope, which gave rise to rumours he had formally to deny, that during that visit he had made arrangements with the Pope to destroy the Irish Church Establishment, and that he was a Roman Catholic in heart.

In 1867 Mr. Disraeli, as leader of the House of Commons, introduced his celebrated Reform Bill, or, rather, Reform Resolutions. He proposed to reduce the occupation franchise for boroughs to a £6 rating, in counties to £20. The franchise was also to be extended to persons having £50 in the funds or £50 in a savings bank for a year. Payment of £20 of direct taxes would also be a title to the franchise, as would a University degree. Votes would further be given to clergymen, ministers of religion generally, members of the learned professions, and certificated schoolmasters. It was proposed to disfranchise Yarmouth, Lancaster, Reigate, and Totnes, and to take one member each from twenty-three boroughs with less than seven thousand inhabitants. The House would have thirty seats to dispose of, and it was proposed to allot fourteen of them to new boroughs in the Northern and Midland districts, fifteen to counties, and one to the London University; the second division of the Tower Hamlets two members, and several new county divisions would have two additional members each. The scheme would add 212,000 voters to the boroughs, and 206,500 to the counties. Mr. Gladstone pointed out the inconvenience of proceeding by resolution, and the Government undertook to introduce a Bill.

In March, 1867, the Bill was introduced, much to the dissatisfaction of Lord Cranborne, now Lord Salisbury, the Earl of Carnarvon, and General Peel, who resigned the offices they held. But the Bill was read a second time without a dissentient; the fight in the Committee was short and sharp. In May Lord Houghton writes: 'I met Gladstone at breakfast. He seemed quite awed with the diabolical wickedness of Dizzy, who, he says, is gradually driving all ideas of political honour out of the House, and accustoming it to the most revolting cynicism.' At this time it is understood that there was a temporary want of harmony between Mr. Gladstone and some of his supporters. When the Bill was read a third time Lord Cranborne denied emphatically that it was a Conservative triumph. The Bill, he said, had been modified at the dictation of Mr. Gladstone, who demanded, first, the lodger franchise; secondly, the abolition of the distinction between compounders and non-compounders; thirdly, a provision to prevent traffic in votes; fourthly, the omission of the taxing franchise; fifthly, the omission of the dual vote; sixthly, the enlargement of the distribution of seats; seventhly, the reduction of the county franchise, the omission of voting-papers, and the omission of the educational and savings banks franchise. 'If,' continued his lordship, 'the adoption of the principles of Mr. Bright could be described as a triumph, then the Conservative party in the whole history of its previous annals had won no such signal triumph before. I desire,' continued Lord Cranbourne, 'to protest in the most earnest language I am capable of against the political morality on which the measures of this year have been passed. If you borrow your politics from the ethics of the political adventurer, you may depend upon it the whole of your political institutions will crumble beneath your feet.' In the House of Lords Earl Derby unblushingly described it as a leap in the dark. Shooting Niagara it was described by Carlyle. Mr. Disraeli, however, rejoiced with exceeding joy over the event. By his own energy and faith in himself he had attained to the highest distinction—yet still many regarded him with distrust. In August Bishop Wilberforce writes: 'No one can even guess at the political future. Whether a fresh election will strengthen the Conservatives or not seems altogether doubtful. The most wonderful thing is the rise of Disraeli.'

At this time Mr. Maurice wrote to his son: 'I am glad you have seen Gladstone, and have been able to judge a little of what his face indicates. It is a very expressive one—hard-worked, as you say; not, perhaps, especially happy; more indicative of struggle than of victory, but not without promise of that. I admire him for his patient attention to details, and for the pains which he takes to prevent himself from being absorbed in them. He has preserved the type which I remember he bore at the University thirty-six years ago, though it has undergone curious developments.'

When in February, 1868, Parliament met, it was announced that Lord Derby, owing to failing health, had resigned—that Mr. Disraeli was to be Premier. And then came Mr. Gladstone's turn. The Liberal party, once more united, had things all their own way. Mr. Gladstone brought in a Bill to abolish compulsory Church rates, and that was carried. He announced that he held the condition of the Irish Church to be unsatisfactory. In March he moved: '1. That in the opinion of this House it is necessary that the Established Church of Ireland should cease to exist as an Establishment, due regard being had for all personal interests and to all individual rights of property. 2. That, subject to the foregoing considerations, it is expedient to prevent the creation of new personal interests by the exercise of any public patronage, and to confine the operations of the Ecclesiastical Commissioners to objects of immediate necessity or involving individual rights, pending the final decision of Parliament. 3. That an humble address be presented to Her Majesty, humbly to pray that, with a view to the purposes aforesaid, Her Majesty will be graciously pleased to place at the disposal of Parliament interest in the temporalities, in archbishoprics, bishoprics, and other ecclesiastical dignities and benefices in Ireland and in the custody thereof.' 'I am sorry,' writes Bishop Wilberforce, 'Mr. Gladstone has moved the attack on the Irish Church. It is altogether a bad business, and I am afraid Gladstone has been drawn into it from the unconscious influence of his restlessness at being out of office. I have no doubt that his hatred to the low tone of the Irish Church has had a great deal to do with it.'

For many years the subject had been before the public. A Royal Commission had been appointed to deal with the question, and it had given rise to more than one debate in the House of Commons. Mr. Gladstone's own adoption of the policy of Disestablishment had been made evident in a speech delivered July, 1867, although he abstained from voting. His relation to the question had, however, as he indicated, been practically declared for more than twenty years. A year later, on a motion by Mr. Maguire, 'that this House resolves itself into a Committee with the view of taking into consideration the condition and circumstances of Ireland,' Mr. Gladstone spoke more decidedly, declaring that, in order to the settlement of the condition of the Irish, the Church as a State Church must cease to exist, and in consequence of this declaration Mr. Maguire withdrew his motion. On the first division on Mr. Gladstone's resolutions he obtained a majority of sixty against Government. Subsequent divisions having confirmed and increased this majority, Mr. Disraeli announced on May 4 that he had advised Her Majesty to dissolve Parliament in the coming autumn, in order that the opinion of the country might be taken on the great issue put before it. Great was the excitement everywhere, and many were the public meetings held on the subject in all parts of England. At a meeting of Church supporters held in St. James's Hall in May, Archbishop Longley in the chair, there were twenty-five bishops on the platform, besides an array of peers and M.P.'s. Archbishop Tait, who moved the first resolution, referring to a speech of his own on the Church Rate Bill, writes to his son: 'Gladstone fell foul of it somewhat roughly on moving his Irish Church resolutions, but last Sunday your mother and I went to the little church in Windmill Street which Mr. Kempe has built for the poor of St. James's, and there found Mr. and Mrs. Gladstone taking refuge from the glare of London for a quiet Sunday morning; and as we all walked home together, I had some most agreeable conversation with him. I wish he was not so strangely impetuous, for he is certainly a good Christian. . . . I almost hope that something may be done to bring him to reason about reforming, not destroying, the Irish Church. This, no doubt, is what the Old Whigs really desire, if only they could get Disraeli out.' Mr. Disraeli soon gratified—at any rate, to a certain extent—the Old Whigs. In November the constituencies replied to the appeal made to them by Mr. Disraeli by an almost unprecedented majority for his opponent. The national verdict could no longer be opposed. Mr. Disraeli himself recognised the fact by resigning office without waiting for the meeting of Parliament. When Parliament met in February, Mr. Gladstone was Premier. Defeated in Lancashire, he had been elected for Greenwich.

There were, of course, party cavillings when the member for Greenwich was gazetted in August, 1873, as Chancellor of the Exchequer without vacating his seat for the Metropolitan borough; but the polemics in the press gradually ceased upon the subject, without materially weakening his influence upon his pledged supporters, and the public at large hardly found time to listen to the controversy. Trade was good, and remunerative enterprise continued to advance by leaps and bounds—to borrow one of Mr. Gladstone's famous phrases. On one occasion, when a Tory member argued against a certain measure that it was not the right time to introduce it, Mr. Bernal Osborne wittily exclaimed: 'Not the right time, sir? We take our time from Greenwich.'

No sooner had Parliament met than the Queen, in order to smooth the difficulties of the question, wrote to Bishop Tait, who had then become Archbishop of Canterbury: 'The Queen has seen Mr. Gladstone, who shows the most conciliatory disposition. He really seems to be moderate in his views, and anxious, so far as he properly and consistently can do so, to meet the wishes of those who would maintain the Irish Church. He at once assured the Queen of his readiness—and, indeed, his anxiety—to meet the Archbishop and to communicate freely with him on the subject of this most important question; and the Queen must express her hope that the Archbishop will meet him in the same spirit.' The Government could do nothing that would tend to raise a suspicion of their sincerity in proposing to disendow the Irish Church, and to withdraw all State endowments from all religious communities in Ireland, but with these conditions accepted, all other matters connected with the question might, the Queen thought, thus become the subject of discussion and negotiation. The interview, when it took place, seems to have much relieved the Archbishop's mind, especially as Mr. Gladstone at that date had not made public any authoritative statement of the shape which his Disestablishment policy was to assume. The Archbishop used to say in after-years that his position after the interview for about ten days was the most difficult he had ever known. In addition to the necessarily urgent correspondence of such a time, he had to grant interviews to men of every sort and condition who came to consult, inform or interrogate him upon the absorbing topic which was on every lip; and he had not merely to give attention to larger comments and conjectures, and to say something suitable in reply, but to keep entirely secret all the while the scheme which Mr. Gladstone had unfolded to him, and even the fact that such a communication had taken place.

At length came Monday, March 1, and Mr. Gladstone unfolded his scheme. For some three hours and a half Mr. Gladstone occupied the attention—the absorbed attention—of an eager House. It was one of his grandest oratorical triumphs. Complicated details, which in other hands would have been dry and lifeless, kept the listener spellbound. 'It was strange,' writes the Archbishop, 'to hear Gladstone on Monday last unfold his scheme in the House of Commons, knowing beforehand what it was all to be, and having, indeed, had a rehearsal of it in my library.'

Mr. Gladstone's Bill was in accordance with the resolutions he had moved when in opposition. The actual moment of Disestablishment he proposed to postpone until January 1, 1871; but from the passing of the Act the creation of private interests was to cease, and the property of the Church was to pass at once into the hands of Commissioners appointed for the purpose. All the ecclesiastical laws of the Disestablished Church were to exist as a binding contract to regulate the internal affairs of the Disestablished Church until such time as they should be altered by the voluntary agency of whatever new governing body would be appointed. The churches and burial-grounds were to become on application the property of the Disestablished Church, and the glebe-houses as well, on payment of the somewhat heavy existing building charges. The whole value of the Church property was estimated at sixteen millions; of this sum, £8,500,000 would be swallowed up in the necessary compensation of various kinds, and the remaining seven and a half millions would be applied to the advantage of the Irish people, but not to Church purposes. Special provision was made for incumbents and unbeneficed curates. As to the post-Reformation grants, Mr. Gladstone fixed a dividing line at the year 1680, agreeing that all grants made from private sources subsequent to that year should be handed over intact to the Disestablished Church. As to the remaining seven millions and a half, it was to be devoted to the relief 'of unavoidable calamities and suffering not provided for by the Poor Law,' to the support of lunatic and idiot asylums, institutions for the relief of the deaf and dumb and blind, and other kindred objects. These details, one after another, were set forth with great clearness, and the speech was closed with a magnificent peroration, which drew a warm tribute of admiration even from the bitterest opponents of the Bill.

In the House of Commons the Bill was carried triumphantly, in spite of good debating on the part of its enemies. On the second reading, the division was 368 for, 250 against. But it was in the Lords that the battle was chiefly fought, when the second reading was carried, after a debate which lasted till three in the morning, by 179 against 146. Upon a division being called, the two English Archbishops, amid a scene of intense excitement, retired to the steps of the throne, which are technically not within the House; Bishop Wilberforce and several Conservative peers withdrew. Among the Conservatives who voted with the Government were Lord Salisbury, Lord Bath, Lord Devon, Lord Carnarvon, and Lord Nelson. The only Bishop who voted with the Government was Bishop Thirlwall, of St. David's. Thirteen English and three Irish Bishops voted on the other side. But in Committee the Lords tacked on sixty-two amendments. Punch had a clever cartoon on the occasion. The Archbishop of Canterbury was represented as a gipsy nurse giving back a changeling instead of the child that had been presented to him, saying, 'Which we've took the greatest care of 'm, ma'm,' while Mrs. the Prime Minister replies, 'This is not my child—not in the least like it.' The Ministerialists described the Bill to be so mutilated as to be practically useless, and the vociferous Radical cheers which greeted Mr. Gladstone as he rose on July 15 to move that the Lords' amendments be considered were significant of the temper of the House. Nothing could be more uncompromising than his speech. He made no attempt to soften down the differences; he even accentuated their gravity, as he recounted the amendments one by one, and called upon the House to reject the preposterous proposals of men who had shown themselves to be as ignorant of the feelings of the country as if they had been 'living in a balloon.' He insisted on the rejection of each and every clause which involved, however indirectly, the proposal of concurrent endowment; he declined to sanction the postponement of the date of Disestablishment; and he declined to leave the disposal of the anticipated surplus to the wisdom of a future Parliament. He consented, however, to allow a reconsideration of the commutation terms, and he went further than some of his supporters in agreeing to give the lump half-million in lieu of the private endowments which had been so much discussed. His unyielding attitude made the Lords furious. When the Peers met, after a debate of quite unusual warmth, they resolved by a majority of 74 to agree to the first and most important of their amendments—the authorization of the principle of concurrent endowments. Lord Granville immediately adjourned the House to take counsel with his colleagues. It seemed as if a collision between the two Houses was inevitable. However, Mr. Gladstone and Lord Cairns met, a compromise was effected, the danger of a collision between the two Houses was avoided, and the Bill for Disestablishing and Disendowing the Irish Church—which Mr. Gladstone had enthusiastically and somewhat sanguinely believed to be a message of peace to Ireland—became law. The Archbishop of Canterbury, who had been one of the chief instruments in the negotiations, writes in his diary: 'We have made the best terms we could, and, thanks to the Queen, a collision between the Houses has been averted; but a great occasion has been poorly used, and the Irish Church has been greatly injured without any benefits to the Roman Catholics.'

In Ireland the scheme was met with mingled emotions. The Church party were in despair, and their attachment to England was undoubtedly weakened. One of the ablest of Irish patriots—Mr. John O'Neill Daunt—wrote: 'The scheme, as set forth, is to some extent undoubtedly a disendowment scheme, but objectionable in not going so far in that direction as Mr. Gladstone might have done with propriety and with full consideration for the vested interests of existing incumbents. His capitation scheme is, in fact, a plan for re-endowment, by which several millions of money, obtained by the sale of Church property, will be permanently abstracted from the Irish public and appropriated to the ecclesiastical uses of the present State Churchmen and their successors. This is anything but equality, and cannot be accepted as a final settlement by the Irish nation.' Again he writes: 'The Lords have passed Mr. Gladstone's Bill, with some mutilations, to which the Commons finally assented in a conference. The Bill is a wretched abortion—in fact, it is such a sham as might have been expected from an English Parliament. It pretends to disendow the State Church, which it re-endows with about five-eighths of the Church property in a capitalized shape. . . . If Gladstone were an honest friend of Ireland, he could have averted all this danger by withholding the power to capitalize. To be sure, it is a queer disendowment that sends off the parsons with five-eighths of the money in their pockets.' Again he writes: 'On the whole, I dare say we have a sort of qualified triumph—nothing to boast of, considering that the result of nearly thirteen years' agitation is a measure that enables the parsons to walk off with ten or eleven millions of our money in their pockets, that still exacts from us the rascally rent-charge, and that swindles Ireland of the amount of Irish taxes heretofore kept in the country by Maynooth and the Regium Donum.'

Nor were the English Dissenters, by whose aid Mr. Gladstone had carried the Bill, very much elated about it. Their organ, the British Quarterly Review, at some length showed how Mr. Gladstone's pretended disendowment had given back the State Church property to the disestablished clergy in a capitalized shape. It was enough for the mob to feel that Mr. Gladstone had put an end to the Irish State Church—that upas-tree which had long blighted the country. Be that as it may, nothing was more beautiful than Mr. Gladstone's peroration when he moved his resolutions. Said he: 'There are many who think that to lay hands on the National

Church Establishment is a profane and unhallowed act. I sympathize with it. I sympathize with it, while I think it is my duty to overcome and suppress it. There is something in the idea of a National Establishment of religion—of a solemn appropriation of a part of the commonwealth for conferring upon all who are ready to receive it what we know to be an inestimable benefit; of saving that part or portion of the inheritance from private selfishness, in order to extract from it, if we can, pure and unmixed advantages of the highest order for the population at large. There is something attractive in this—so attractive that it is an image that must always command the homage of the many. It is somewhat like the kingly ghost in "Hamlet," of which one of the characters of Shakespeare says:

But, sir, this is to view a religious Establishment upon one side only—upon what I may call the ethereal side; it has likewise a side of earth. And here I cannot do better than quote some lines written by the present Archbishop of Dublin at a time when his genius was devoted to the Muses. He said, speaking of mankind:

And so the Church Establishment, regarded in its theory and its aim, is beautiful and attractive. Yet what is it but an appropriation of public property—an appropriation of the fruits of labour and skill to certain purposes; and unless those purposes are fulfilled, that appropriation cannot be justified. Therefore, sir, I think we must set aside fears, which thrust themselves upon the imagination, and act upon the sober dictates of our judgment. I think it has been shown that the cause for action is strong—not for precipitate action, not for action beyond our powers, but for such action as the opportunities of the times and the condition of Parliament, if there is a ready will, will amply and easily admit of. If I am asked as to my expectations of the issue of this struggle, I begin by frankly avowing that I, for one, would not have entered into it unless I had believed that the final hour was about to sound. "Venit summa dies et ineluctabile fatum." And I hope that the noble lord will forgive me if I say that before last Friday I thought that the thread of the remaining life of the Irish Established Church was short, but that since Friday last, when at half-past four o'clock in the afternoon the noble lord stood at that table, I have regarded it as being shorter still. The issue is not in our hands. What we had and have to do is to consider deeply and well before we take the first step in an engagement such as this, but, having entered into the controversy, there and then to acquit ourselves like men, and to use every effort to remove what still remains of the scandals and calamities in the relations that exist between England and Ireland, and to make our best efforts, at least, to fill up with the cement of human concord the noble fabric of the British Empire.'

Mr. Gladstone triumphed. Mr. Disraeli contented himself with the victory of his great rival. Mr. M'Cullagh Torrens writes that he happened to pass near the Conservative leader in the cloisters as he muffled to resist the outer air, and could not help asking him what he thought of Gladstone's speech in introducing the Bill. 'Oh,' he said, 'perfectly wonderful! Nobody but himself could have gone through such a mass of statistics, history, and computations.' And then, after a pause: 'And so characteristic in the finish to throw away the surplus on the other idiots.'

CHAPTER IX. EDUCATION AND IRELAND.

During the Educational debates Mr. Miall said that the Premier had 'led one section of the Liberal party through the valley of humiliation; but once bit, twice shy, and we can't stand this sort of thing much longer.' Mr. Gladstone sharply replied: 'I hope that my hon. friend will not continue his support of the Government one moment longer than he deems it consistent with his sense of duty and right. For God's sake, sir, let him withdraw it the moment he thinks it better for the cause he has at heart that he should do so. So long as my hon. friend thinks fit to give us his support, we will co-operate with my hon. friend for any purpose we have in common, but when we think his opinions and demands exacting, when we think that he looks too much to the section of the community he adorns, and too little to the interests of the people at large, we must then recollect that we are the Government of the Queen, and that those who have assumed the high responsibility of administering the affairs of the empire must endeavour to forget the part in the whole, and must, in the great measures they introduce into the House, propose to themselves no meaner or narrower object—no other object than the welfare of the empire at large.' Again, in opposing Mr. Miall's motion for doing to the English Church what had been done to the Irish, he said: 'The Church of England is not a foreign Church; it is the growth of the history and traditions of the country. It is not the number of its members or the millions of its revenue—it is the mode in which it has been from a period shortly after the Christian era, and has never for 1,300 years ceased to be, the Church of the country, having been at every period engrained into the hearts and feelings of the great mass of the people, and having entwined itself with the local habits and feelings, so that I do not believe there lives the man who could either divine the amount and character of the work my honourable friend would have to undertake were he doomed to be responsible for the execution of his own propositions, or who could in the least degree define or anticipate the consequences by which it would be attended. If Mr. Miall sought to convert the majority of the House of Commons to his views, he must begin by converting to his views the opinions of the majority of the people of England.'

The attempt to carry an Irish University Bill led Mr. Gladstone to resign. Mr. W. E. Forster writes: 'Gladstone rose with the House dead against him, and made a wonderful speech, easy— almost playful—with passages of great power and eloquence, but with a graceful ease which enabled him to plant daggers into Horsman, Fitzmaurice and Co.' Again he writes: 'Gladstone determined to resign; outside opinion very strongly for resignation. Gladstone made quite a touching little speech; he began playfully. This was the last of a hundred Cabinets, and he wished to say to his colleagues with what profound gratitude—and then he broke down, and could only say that he would not enter on the details. Tears came into my eyes, and we were all very touched.' As Mr. Disraeli was unable to form a Government, Mr. Gladstone, however, soon returned to power, he resuming his old place as Chancellor of the Exchequer. Touching the Irish University Bill, Lord Blachford writes: 'Coleridge is sanguine about Gladstone's Irish University Bill. He seems to have started with the Cabinet against him, and to have converted them all (their point being, I suppose, to have something that would pass), especially some whom

Coleridge describes as full of admiration for the scheme. I don't understand it, but I imagine that it gives or leaves to everybody enough to stop their mouths without infuriating their neighbours.' As stated, Mr. Gladstone returned to office, only to leave it in the following year, when he dissolved Parliament and the Tories had a majority. Mr. Gladstone retained his seat for Greenwich, but a local Tory was at the head of the poll.

Lord Russell's charges against Mr. Gladstone of indifference on colonial questions is somewhat borne out by his conduct with regard to the annexation of Fiji, which he opposed in 1873, but which was ultimately carried out by the Government that succeeded his in the following year. In reply to Sir W. M'Arthur's motion in the House for the annexation of Fiji, Mr. Gladstone said: 'Nothing was easier than to make out a plausible case of appropriation of this kind, and yet nothing would so much excite the displeasure of those who cheered his honourable friend the member for Lambeth, than when for such appropriations a similar disposition was shown by other countries. It might be the chill of old age that was coming upon him, but he confessed he did not feel that excitement for the acquisition of new territory which animated the hon. gentleman.' As to commerce, with our inability 'to cope with expanding opportunities, he did not feel the pressure of the argument for securing special guarantees for our trade in every part of the world.' He was more discursive in replying to what he called, 'in no taunting spirit, the philanthropic part of the question.'

Nothing was more unexpected, or, as it happened, nothing more disastrous, than Mr. Gladstone's sudden dissolution of Parliament in 1874. Mr. M'Cullagh Torrens writes: 'On January 24 I was amused at breakfast by a paragraph read by one of my family—which, in the profundity of legislative wisdom, I treated as an editorial jest—announcing an immediate dissolution. When convinced at last by reference to an address to Greenwich that the decree had really gone forth, my breath was again taken away by learning that the immediate cause was the authoritative confession that the Cabinet had lost the necessary influence in directing public opinion, and that the new departure requisite for its recovery consisted in the offer to abolish the income-tax, and the creation of a number of peasant boroughs instead of those which might be still spared as belonging to the upper classes.' Mr. Chamberlain severely described Mr. Gladstone's address containing these proposals as 'the meanest public document which had ever in like circumstances proceeded from a statesman of the first rank.' It fell flat on the public.

In 1875 Mr. Gladstone, to the surprise of his friends, announced his determination to retire from the leadership of his party, and the Marquis of Hartington was selected in his stead, and held that post until the end of the session of 1879. The situation was a little embarrassing. The difficulties he had to encounter as leader of a minority in the House of Commons were enormously increased by the fact that he had to deal, not merely with his followers, but with his brilliant predecessor, who could at any moment, by his own individual action, lead the Liberal party into any course in which he chose to direct them.

Continuing his career as a reformer, we find Mr. Gladstone repealing the Ecclesiastical Titles Bill, and abolishing religious tests in the Universities; and as the Lords threw out his Bill for the Abolition of Purchase in the Army, he abolished it by Royal Warrant. Many old Whigs questioned the wisdom of the procedure, as they did also his conduct in the Alabama Claims, which he referred to arbitration, when, as is always the case, the arbitrators decided against us and in favour of America. Earl Russell, who has a claim to be heard on the question, writes that he declined to submit the claims to arbitration by a foreign Power because 'it appeared to me that we could not consistently with our position as an independent State allow a foreign Power to decide either that Great Britain had been wanting in good faith or that our law officers did not understand so well as a foreign Power or State the meaning of a British statute.'

His lordship severely criticised the way in which Mr. Gladstone formed his Ministry, as done with little tact or discrimination. 'I cannot think,' he continues, 'that I was mistaken in giving way to Mr. Gladstone as head of the Whig-Radical party of England. During Lord Palmerston's Ministry I had every reason to admire the boldness and the judgment with which he had directed our finances. I had no reason to suppose that he was less attached than I was to our national honour; that he was less proud than I was of our national achievements by land or sea; that he disliked the extension of our colonies; or that his measures would tend to reduce the great and glorious empire of which he was put in charge to a manufactory of cheap cloth and a market for cheap goods, with an army and navy reduced by paltry savings to a standard of weakness and inefficiency.'

In March, 1874, Mr. Gladstone addressed a letter to Lord Granville, in which he said: 'At my age I must reserve my entire freedom to divest myself of all the responsibilities of leadership at no distant date. . . . I should be desirous shortly before the season of 1874 to consider whether there would not be an advantage in my placing my services for a time at the disposal of the Liberal party, or whether I should claim exemption from the duties I have hitherto discharged.' Mr. Gladstone at that time was sixty-four—certainly no great age for himself or any other statesman of his time; and when Mr. Russell Gurney proposed to legislate on Ritualism, Mr. Gladstone was back in the field. After his unsuccessful intervention, Mr. Gladstone again retired from active participation in affairs; but he returned to the subject in the autumn by contributing an article to the Contemporary Review, in which he passionately protested against the attempt to impose uniformity of practice on the clergy of the Church of England by legislation. In the following passage he did much to offend the Roman Catholics: 'As to the question whether a handful of clergy are or are not engaged in an utterly hopeless and visionary attempt to Romanize the Church and the people of England, at no time since the bloody reign of Queen Mary has such a scheme been possible. But if it had been possible in the seventeenth or eighteenth centuries, it would still have become impossible in the nineteenth, when Rome has substituted for the proud boast of semper eadem a policy of violence and change in faith; when she has refurbished every rusty weapon she was fondly thought to have disused; when no one can become her convert without renouncing his mental and moral freedom, and placing his civil loyalty and duty at the mercy of another; and when she has equally repudiated modern thought and ancient history.' This article was followed up by his celebrated pamphlet, 'The Vatican Decrees in their bearing on Civil Allegiance.'

Ministers had an easy time of it till they got to the purchase of the shares in the Suez Canal, which Mr. Gladstone vehemently opposed, though it seems to have turned out well. When Mr. Gladstone declared that it was an unprecedented thing to spend the money of the nation in that way, Sir Stafford Northcote replied: 'So is the canal.' Mr. Gladstone was soon to prove how far from real was his intention of retiring into private life. We began to hear of Bulgarian atrocities and of the Turkish horrors. It was a cause into which Mr. Gladstone threw himself heart and soul. He published an article in the Contemporary Review, advocating the expulsion of 'the unspeakable Turk,' bag and baggage, from the country. His pamphlets were in every hand. In the meanwhile we had another crisis in the East. We were on the verge of war with Russia, and the Jingoes, as the war party came to be denominated, went about the streets singing:

Mr. Disraeli had sought refuge in the House of Lords as Earl Beaconsfield. All this time Mr. Gladstone kept rather quiet in Parliament, but from time to time he addressed meetings in the country, denouncing the Jingoes. We find him, however, supporting a vote of censure on the Government, moved by Lord Hartington, he himself having already moved one. It was a false move in tactics, as the Government obtained a crushing majority. But the Ministry were doomed, nevertheless. At the General Election in 1880 they had a decisive defeat, mainly due to Mr. Gladstone, who had gone to Scotland to win Midlothian, hitherto the stronghold of the Duke of Buccleugh, and who had carried the fiery cross in triumph from London to the North. Never had he exerted himself more, and never with such splendid results. As Mr. Disraeli had said when referring to Mr. Gladstone's temporary retirement from political life, 'There will be a return from Elba;' nor was that return long delayed. Once more he was Premier.

But there was a difficulty. At the time of the victory Lord Hartington, not Mr. Gladstone, was the leader of the Liberal party. When Lord Beaconsfield resigned, which he had the grace to do without meeting Parliament, the Queen, according to precedent, sent for Lord Hartington. He could do nothing, and then the Queen summoned Lord Granville, the Liberal leader in the Lords. The two statesmen went together to the Queen, and assured her that the victory was Mr. Gladstone's, and that he was the only possible Premier. They returned to London in the afternoon, and called upon Mr. Gladstone in Harley Street. He was expecting the message which they brought, and he went down to Windsor without a moment's delay. This was on April 23. That evening he kissed hands and returned to London, a second time Premier. The prospect was not cheering. On a vote on the Bradlaugh affair the Government majority was seventy-five. There were difficulties about Sir Bartle Frere at the Cape, about Cyprus, about the Employers' Liability Bill, and a hot debate on opium. 'Gladstone,' writes Sir Stafford Northcote, 'had been dining out to meet the authoress of "Sister Dora" (Miss Lonsdale), who was very much alarmed by the rapidity and variety of his questions, and only came back in time to express his opinion that the House was too much influenced by sentiment and too little by judgment. It must be as good as a play to hear such sentiments from such a quarter.' In the course of one of the debates on the Bradlaugh affair, Sir Stafford Northcote writes: 'Gladstone spoke early, and evidently under great anxiety. His speech, especially in the earlier part, was a very fine one, and produced a considerable impression. Towards the end, however, he refined too much, and seemed a little to lose his hold of his audience. Gibson followed him with a very able and telling speech, but, unfortunately, the House had greatly emptied for dinner when Mr. Gladstone sat down. It is a favourite habit of his to speak into the dinner-hour, so that his opponent must speak either to empty benches or forego the advantage of replying on the instant.' The Opposition when the division was taken had a majority of forty-four, 'a result,' adds Sir Stafford Northcote, 'wholly unexpected on our side, the more sanguine having only hoped for a close run, and being prepared to renew the fight by moving the previous question, and adjourning the debate on it. The excitement when the numbers were given was greater than I ever remember. There was shouting, cheering, clapping of hands, and other demonstrations, both louder and longer than any I ever heard in my Parliamentary life.'

It may be stated that ultimately the question of Bradlaugh was settled by Mr. Gladstone's moving a resolution to admit all persons who may claim their right to do so, without question and subject to their liability to penalties by the State.

When the new Parliament assembled the Liberals were in a majority of more than a hundred, if the Irish Home Rulers were counted as neutral. If they were added to the Liberal ranks, their majority became 170. No one then thought of adding them to the Conservatives, though half of them—the Parnellites—subsequently voted with the Conservatives in a vast number of divisions, and finally contributed to Mr. Gladstone's downfall.

CHAPTER X. IRELAND UNDER MR. FORSTER.

When Mr. Gladstone returned to power, Mr. Forster was appointed Chief Secretary for Ireland, with Lord Cowper as Viceroy. There was great distress—as there generally is in Ireland—and exceptional efforts had been made, both by the Government and the people of this country, to meet it. A benevolent fund had been raised, chiefly through the influence of the Duchess of Marlborough, wife of the Lord-Lieutenant, and a Distress Relief Act had been carried by Parliament to empower the application of three-quarters of a million of the Irish Church Surplus Fund, and some good had unquestionably been done by the public and private effort thus made to relieve distress; but it was clear, from the results of the elections, and from the speeches of the popular Irish leaders, that it was not to measures of this kind that the people looked for permanent relief. The unusual distress of 1879 had intensified and aggravated the chronic disaffection, and sixty members had been returned to Parliament who were pledged to do their utmost to put an end to English rule in Ireland by securing Home Rule. Flushed with the brilliant success they had achieved, the Liberal party entered upon office confident that a career of prosperity lay before them. Lord Beaconsfield's defeat had been brought about by the national repudiation of his foreign policy; and, in the first instance, it was of foreign, rather than domestic, affairs that the new House of Commons was thinking. But Ireland at once came to the front. The existing Coercion Act would expire in a few weeks, and it was necessary to secure its renewal before it lapsed; but the Cabinet resolved to try the experiment of governing by means of the ordinary law.

The Lords threw out Mr. Forster's measures intended to relieve Ireland. He did not scruple to avow his vexation and resentment at their summary rejection, and the dangerous effect it would have in the disturbed districts during the coming winter, which might lead to the adoption of much stronger measures, both of concession and coercion, than the Government had hitherto attempted. In response, Mr. Parnell, in addressing a great audience at Ennis, enunciated the plan already known as boycotting, whereby every man who took an evicted farm, and everyone who aided or abetted eviction, should be shunned as a leper in the fair, refused custom in the market, and treated as an intruder at the altar. Before the year was out the courts established by the Land League publicly heard and determined the merits of each case as it arose. The signal for acts of summary violence was set by the fate of Lord Mountmorres, who had incurred popular dislike by his conduct as a rigorous magistrate, and was put to death on the highway near his own house in open daylight. Mr. Forster early proposed to suspend the Habeas Corpus Act, and to prosecute the prominent movers of the agitation. Mr. Gladstone clung to the hope that the friends of law and order would combine to suppress the tendencies to outrage, and wished to defer as long as possible the suspension of constitutional freedom; but ere Parliament had reassembled in 1881, the progress of disorder and outrage had increased, and the Cabinet reluctantly authorized the introduction of a measure for the protection of life and property. Twenty-two nights were spent in debating it; but it was passed by an overwhelming majority, comprising Ministerialists, Radicals, and Conservatives. But the obstruction systematically offered to repressive legislation at last provoked Speaker Brand to assert a discretionary power of terminating debate, which led to the introduction of a change of procedure, of which the most prominent measure was the Clôture.

The Irish Land Bill was the chief work of the session of 1881. Mr. Forster's work at this time was arduous and untiring to keep the Cabinet up to duty. In October, 1881, Mr. Gladstone writes from Hawarden: 'Your sad and saddening letter supplies much food for serious reflection; but I need not reply at great length, mainly because I practically agree with you. I almost take for granted, and I shall assume until you correct me, that your meaning about ruin to property is as follows: You do not mean the ruin to property which may directly result from exclusive dealing, but you mean ruin to property by violence—e.g., burning of a man's haystack because he had let his cars on hire to the constabulary. On this assumption I feel politically quite prepared to concur with you in acting upon legal advice to this effect; nor do I dissent, under the circumstances, from the series of propositions by which you seek to connect Parnell and Co. with the prevalent intimidation. But I hardly think that so novel an application of the Protection Act should be undertaken without the Cabinet.'

In the same month Mr. Gladstone went to Leeds, where he had a reception which exceeded all expectations. In his speech he devoted himself to the Irish Question. Amidst enthusiastic cheers from the vast audience, he pointed to Mr. Forster's name, and spoke in generous terms of the arduous and painful task in which he was then engaged; and then he went on in clear and forcible language to denounce the conduct of Mr. Parnell and of the other Land League leaders in striving to stand between the people of Ireland and the Land Act, in order that the beneficial effects of that measure might not be allowed to reach them. Such conduct, Mr. Gladstone declared, would not be tolerated. 'The resources of civilization were,' he observed, 'not exhausted.' Then followed the arrest of Mr. Parnell. Within twelve hours the news was spread over the civilized world, and everywhere it created a great sensation. Mr. Gladstone, speaking at a meeting at the Guildhall on the same day, first announced the fact of Mr. Parnell's arrest to the people of England, and the statement was received with an enthusiastic outburst that startled even the speaker himself. It was hailed as if it were the news of a signal victory. Throughout England the belief—so soon to be dissipated—was held that the imprisonment of Mr. Parnell at Kilmainham must mean the downfall of his authority, and the extinction of the great organization of which he was the head; in reality, the outrages and assassinations became greater.

One result was a change in the policy of the Government. The English public was asked to believe that the Irish policy of the Government was not the policy of Mr. Gladstone, but of Mr. Forster alone. On March 24, 1882, Mr. Gladstone wrote to Mr. Forster, who was then in Dublin, pointing out to him the growing opposition to the Ministerial proposals for instituting the Closure, and the prevalent belief among the Irish members in the House that by stopping the Closure they might prevent the renewal of the Protection Act. The Prime Minister added 'that, with the Land Act working briskly, resistance to process disappearing, and rents increasingly and even generally, though not uniformly, paid, a renewal of so odious a power as that we now hold is impossible, and that whatever may be needed by way of supplement to the ordinary law must be found in other forms.'

Mr. Parnell, speaking at Wexford on October 10, 1881, said: 'He (Mr. Gladstone) would have you believe that he is not afraid of you, because he has disarmed you, because he has attempted to disorganize you, because he knows that the Irish nation is to-day disarmed as far as physical weapons go, but he does not hold this kind of language with the Boers (cheers for the Boers. A Voice: 'We will be Boers too!'). What did he do at the commencement of the session? He said something of this kind with regard to the Boers. He said that he was going to put them down, and as soon as he discovered that they were able to shoot straighter than his own soldiers, he allowed those few men to put him and his Government down, and although he has attempted to regain some of his lost position in the Transvaal by subsequent chicanery and diplomatic negotiations, yet that sturdy and small people in the distant Transvaal have seen through William Ewart Gladstone; and they have told him again, for the second time, that they will not have their liberties filched from them; and I believe that, as a result, we shall see that William Ewart Gladstone will again yield to the people of the Transvaal (hear, hear). And I trust that, as the result of this great movement, we shall see that, just as Gladstone by the Act of 1881 has eaten all his old words, has departed from all his formerly declared principles, now we shall see that these brave words of this English Prime Minister will be scattered as chaff before the united and advancing determination of the Irish people to regain for themselves their lost land and their lost legislative independence (loud and continued cheering).'

Miss Parnell termed him a hoary-headed old miscreant; Miss Helen Taylor, of the London School Board, described him as a dastard and a recreant; Mr. O'Donnell, M.P., said Gladstone was a Judas, who had betrayed Ireland by the kiss of peace to the persecutor and tormentor. In Philadelphia, the City of Brotherly Love, the effigy of Mr. Gladstone was burned by a crowd of fifteen hundred Irish under the direction of the League leaders. Even in Hawarden the magistrates had to place four additional constables to protect Mr. Gladstone from the effects of Irish revenge. Mr. Gladstone, said Mr. Parnell at Wexford just before he was arrested, was the greatest coercionist, the greatest and most unrivalled slanderer of the Irish nation, that ever lived.

The situation was gloomy. Naturally Mr. Gladstone made as light as possible of the situation in the speech he delivered at the Lord Mayor's banquet. The speech for the moment silenced the murmurs of dissension inside the Cabinet. 'You said,' Mr. Gladstone wrote to Forster, 'that if we are to ask for a suspension of Habeas Corpus, it must be on a case of great strength and clearness. But do these figures, after all the allowance to be made for protection, indicate such a case? As far as I can judge, there is a tendency in Ireland upon a series of years to a decline in the total number of homicides. The immense increase in property offences, agrarian, for 1880 seems to me to mark the true character of the crisis and the true source of the mischief of the Land League. But I incline to assume that any suspension of Habeas Corpus must be founded on danger to life.'

When Parliament met in 1881 began the long running fight between Mr. Forster and Mr. Parnell. As the chief representative of the Land League, Mr. Parnell had spoken defending the action of the League, and Mr. Forster retorted that the meetings of that body had constantly been followed by outrage, and that the object of the Land Leaguers was not to bring about an alteration in the law of the land by constitutional means, but to prevent any payment of rent save such as might be in accordance with the unwritten law of Mr. Parnell. In Parliament Government carried a Protection Act, an Arms Bill, and an Irish Land Bill. The Acts were of no avail. Outrages increased after the passing of the Protection Act. In May Mr. John Dillon was arrested and others of his party. In September it was resolved to arrest Mr. Parnell, 'the uncrowned king,' as his followers called him. Mr. Gladstone assented to the arrest if in the opinion of the law officers of the Crown he had by his speeches been guilty of treasonable practices.

On one occasion, when Mr. Forster had suggested that he had better retire, Mr. Gladstone wrote by return of post to acknowledge 'the very grave letter,' which he thought ought to be laid before the Cabinet. 'With regard to your leaving Ireland,' wrote the Prime Minister, 'there is an analogy between your position and mine. Virtually abandoning the hope of vital change for the better, I come on my own behalf to an anticipation projected a little further into the future—that after the winter things may mend, and that my own retirement may give facilities for the fulfilment of your very natural desire.' It was in a day or two after this Mr. Gladstone congratulated Forster upon the manner in which he had accomplished a difficult and delicate task in connection with the Irish Executive. 'It is not every man,' he writes, 'who in difficult circumstances can keep a cool head with a warm heart—and that is what you are doing.'

In 1882 the situation in Ireland became increasingly difficult and dangerous. As the time drew near for the meeting of Parliament, it was evident that the session would be a stormy one. In all quarters attacks upon the Chief Secretary seemed to be in course of preparation. The Protection Act had not put an end to the outrages, despite the fact that hundreds of prisoners, including Mr. Parnell and other members of Parliament, were under lock and key. Above all, the Protection Act would expire during the year, and consequently Ministers must allow it to expire, or must ask Parliament to spend weeks, or possibly months, in renewing it. Yet in the Queen's Speech it was stated that the condition of Ireland showed signs of improvement, and encouraged the hope that perseverance in the course hitherto pursued would be rewarded with the happy results which were so much to be desired. The Lords resolved to find fault with the working of the Land Act. The challenge of the Lords was taken up by the Government in the House of Commons, and a resolution moved by Mr. Gladstone, that any inquiry at that time into the working of the Land Act would defeat its operation, and must be injurious to the interests of good government in Ireland, was carried by a majority of 303 to 235.

After the Easter recess the attacks on Forster were renewed. It was demanded that he should be removed from office, and that the suspects should be immediately released, on the plea that their imprisonment had not prevented the continuance of the outrages. To make matters worse, the American Government became urgent in their demands for the release of those prisoners who could prove that they were citizens of the United States, while, in addition to the political perplexities thus created, the atrocious murder of Mrs. H. J. Smythe, as she was driving home from church in West Meath, sent a thrill of horror through the country. At this time Forster, in a letter to Mr. Gladstone, writes: 'That if now or at any future time' (the Pall Mall had been suggesting his resignation) 'you think that from any cause it would be to the advantage of the public service or for the good of Ireland that I should resign, I most unreservedly place my resignation in your hands.'

In reply, Mr. Gladstone wrote from Hawarden, April 5, 1882: 'Yesterday morning I was unwell, and did not see the papers, so that I have only just become aware of the obliging suggestion that you should retire. I suspect it is partly due to a few (not many) Tory eulogies. There is one consideration which grievously tempts me towards the acceptance of the offer conveyed in your most handsome letter. It is that if you go, and go on Irish grounds, surely I must go too. . . . We must continue to face our difficulties with an unbroken front and with a stout heart. I do not admit your failure, and I think you have admitted it rather too much—at any rate, by omission—by not putting forward the main fact that in the deadly fight with the social revolution you have not failed, but are succeeding. Your failure, were it true, is our failure; and outrage, though a grave fact, is not the main one. Were there a change in the features of the case, I would not hesitate to recognise it, with whatever pain, as unreservedly as I now record their actual condition. I do not suppose we ought to think of legislating on the Irish case until after Whitsuntide.'

But, nevertheless, Mr. Forster did resign. In April Lord Spencer succeeded Earl Cowper as Irish Viceroy, and negotiations were carried on between Captain O'Shea and Mr. Parnell—known now as the Kilmainham Treaty—of which Mr. Forster strongly complained. Mr. Gladstone took a different view. Writing to Forster, he expressed the satisfaction with which he had read Mr. Parnell's letter. With regard to the expression in the letter of the writer's willingness to co-operate in future with the Liberal party, Mr. Gladstone wrote: 'This is a hors d'œuvre which we had no right to expect. I may be far wide of the mark, but I can scarcely wonder at O'Shea saying, "The thing is done. . . ." On the whole, Parnell's letter is the most extraordinary I ever read. I cannot help feeling indebted to O'Shea.'

In May Mr. Forster resigned. Writing on the 2nd of that month, Mr. Gladstone, in reply, says: 'I have received your letter with much grief, but on this it would be selfish to expatiate. I have no choice—followed or not followed, I must go on. . . . One thing, however, I wish to say. You wish to minimize in any public statement the cause of your retreat. In my opinion, and I speak from experience, viewing the nature of the case, you will find this hardly possible. For a justification, I fear, you will have to found upon the doctrine of a new departure, or must protest against it and deny it with heart and soul.'

Speaking of the parting, Mr. Forster told his biographer that he had learned not merely to esteem, but to love Mr. Gladstone during their intercourse as colleagues, and he bore testimony to the fact that he had never ceased to be supported by him until the moment came when the Prime Minister found reason to change his policy. Then, however, the change of policy was swiftly followed by a change of attitude, so far as politics were concerned, deplored by both men, but, under the circumstances, inevitable.

Lord Frederick Cavendish was gazetted as Mr. Forster's successor. He arrived in Dublin on

May 6. On that day he and Mr. Burke, the Irish Under-Secretary, were foully murdered while crossing the Phœnix Park by a band of assassins, whose plans, it was evident, had been laid long beforehand with the utmost deliberation. Mr. Forster had escaped them on his departure from Dublin by what almost seemed a miracle. In a few days after, Sir William Harcourt introduced into the House of Commons a new Coercion Bill, which, although it was laid upon the lines introduced by Mr. Forster before he retired from office, was in many respects more severe and stringent in its character than anything which he had proposed.

Another difficulty which beset the Government was the occupation of Egypt in 1882. The bombardment of Alexandria led to the retirement of Mr. Bright from the Cabinet. Many Liberals were profoundly dissatisfied. In the early part of the session of 1883, the question of our obligations in South Africa, and our duties towards native chiefs who had trusted in our promises, arose in connection with Bechuanaland. In domestic politics the question was that of the Household Suffrage Bill, which, carried in the Commons, was thrown out in the House of Lords.

But a greater question was that of the abandonment of the Soudan and the failure to relieve Gordon at Khartoum. It was in the course of one of his most urgent appeals to Government not to delay the sending out of an expedition that Forster used words respecting Mr. Gladstone which were strangely misinterpreted at the time. Speaking of the dangers of Gordon's position, he said: 'I believe everyone but the Prime Minister is already convinced of that danger . . . and I attribute his not being convinced to his wonderful power of persuasion. He can persuade most people of most things, and above all, he can persuade himself of almost anything.' It is difficult now to realize that these words were resented by Lord Hartington as 'a bitter and personal, and evidently highly-prepared and long-reflected-over, attack upon the sincerity of Mr. Gladstone.' It is to be remembered that at this time Mr. Bright had resigned office, and the Government was daily growing weaker. The attack of the Tories was incessant, and the supporters of the Government became daily more faint-hearted. It is said of one of our months that it comes in like a lion and goes out like a lamb. In the present instance this was specially true of the Gladstone Government. In June, 1883, the Government were beaten on the Budget. In reference to this event Lord Shaftesbury writes: 'I have just seen the defeat of Government on the Budget by Conservatives and Parnellites combined; an act of folly amounting to wickedness. God is not in all their thoughts, nor their country either. All seek their own, and their own is party spirit, momentary triumph, political hatred, and the indulgence of low political and unpatriotic passions.'

A more accurate observer, 'I rather fancy,' wrote Mr. W. H. Smith, M.P., 'the Government look for it as a relief from their troubles.' The last, and perhaps the most serious of all, was the manner in which they had allowed themselves to be outwitted by Russia in Afghanistan. This belief was generally entertained all over the land. Mr. Gladstone was glad to put an end to his perplexities by resigning office. The Queen offered to make him an Earl, which he had too much sense to accept—though in office no one was more ready to make peers of his friends. In his later years his trump card was an attack on the House of Lords. Lord Salisbury became Premier, all necessary business was quickly disposed of, and in the autumn a General Election took place. In the boroughs the Liberal losses were heavy; in the counties they increased their strength. One of Mr. Gladstone's appeals to the country was sounded in his speech at Edinburgh to the electors of Midlothian. He passionately implored his party to hold together, in order, above all things, that they should return a Liberal majority so considerable as to make it independent of the Irish party. He expressed the hope that from one end of the country to the other there would not be a single representative returned to Parliament who would listen to any proposition tending to impair the visible empire. Whatever demands might be made on the part of Ireland, if they were to be entertained they must be subject to the condition that the union of the empire should be preserved. Mr. Parnell's answer was to return eighty-six Home-Rulers for Ireland; Lord Salisbury remained Premier. Lord Shaftesbury wrote: 'In a year or so we shall have Home Rule disposed of at all hazards to save us from hourly and daily bores.' In the meanwhile the Conservatives held feebly to office till 1886, when in January Mr. Gladstone resumed office as Premier.

CHAPTER XI. HOME RULE.

About this time Home Rule began seriously to be talked about. It was even hinted that Mr. Gladstone was about to bring in a measure on the subject. In some quarters it was hinted the Conservatives would outbid him in their eagerness to obtain Irish support. Men who belonged to no party could not bring themselves to regard any measure of Home Rule seriously, especially when they saw how by means of it Irish M.P.'s had gained a popularity and a position which otherwise they would never have hoped to attain. An Irish Nationalist had everything to lose by means of a peaceful solution of Irish difficulties—his claim on the funds collected largely in America, his place in Parliament, his position on the public platform. As long as he could teach his ignorant fellow-countrymen and sympathizing Americans that England was the sworn foe of Ireland and did all she could to crush her and keep her down, he had an easy time of it. To abuse England was to play an easy part, and no misrepresentation was too absurd to be put forth to arouse Irish hatred—on which the Catholic priests naturally looked with no unfriendly eyes. For England was a country rich and prosperous and Protestant, and they dared not tell the Irish people that if they copied England Ireland would be as prosperous as any part of Great Britain. Take the case of Mr. Forster, savagely execrated as 'Buckshot' Forster. Why was he held up to hatred under that name? Simply for the reason that buckshot not being so fatal as bullets, Mr. Forster had recommended it to the troops in case they should be obliged to resort to arms. The plain Englishman, aware how for fifty years Parliament had been trying to pacify Ireland and to remove wrong where it was admitted to exist, who heard Irishmen declare that they were at war with England, could not be expected strongly to support a movement in favour of Home Rule, especially after Mr. Gladstone's appeal to him to give him a majority independent of the Irish vote.

Many prejudices had to be overcome. As a rule, the Englishman has slight confidence in Irish oratory. An amusing illustration of its tendency to run into exaggeration is given by that sturdy Irish patriot Mr. John O'Neill Daunt, who in 1882 thus closes his diary for the year: 'The year now ending has been blackened by most abominable crimes and murders. Parnell and his followers acquired vast popularity by denouncing the evictors, the extortioners, the rack-renters; had they stopped there they would have merited praise. But in attacking all landlords—good and bad landlords—they fatally widened that severance of classes which has always been the curse of Ireland.'

Unprejudiced Englishmen—not excited by hope of triumph for a party—were naturally sceptical about Home Rule for Ireland. The masses were quite content to follow Mr. Gladstone's lead, and to applaud the Irish orators who from time to time appeared in their midst. As a nation, the Irish are oratorical and poetical. It is by poetry and oratory the Irishman makes his way in the world, and wins fame and fortune; while the Saxon is content to make a fortune by honest industry and commercial enterprise. An Irish poet—one of the most popular of them perhaps—who is more honoured in England than in the land of his birth, wrote:

And they are content to plod on, while the Irishman revels in the excitement of agitation. But

Mr. Gladstone's new policy was to put down agitation, to satisfy his Irish supporters, and to send another message of peace to Ireland by carrying a measure of Home Rule. His initial difficulty was with his Cabinet. The Marquis of Hartington, Lord Derby, Lord Selborne stood aloof, Mr. Chamberlain and Mr. Trevelyan remaining with him. Early in the session Mr. Gladstone announced that he hoped to be able to lay before the House his plan for the future government of Ireland. Sir Stafford Northcote saw dangers ahead. In a speech he made at Aberdeen, he said of his old leader: 'I am prepared from a long acquaintance with him, both as a friend and as an opponent in Parliament, to bear the highest tribute to the great ability of the late Premier; at the same time, I think he is about the most dangerous statesman I know. . . . It always seems to me that the worst sign of bad weather is when you see the new moon with what is called the old moon in its arms. I have no doubt that many of you Aberdeen men have read the fine old ballad of Sir Patrick Spens, who was drowned some twenty or thirty miles to the east of Aberdeen. In that ballad he was cautioned not to go to sea, because his old and weatherwise attendant had noticed the new moon with the old moon in its lap. I think myself that is a very dangerous sign; and when I see Mr. Chamberlain with Mr. Gladstone, the old moon, in his arms, I think it is time to look out for squally weather.'

Squally weather it was at any rate the misfortune of Mr. Gladstone to encounter in his new endeavour. There was at this time no one in the ranks of the Opposition at all approaching Lord Randolph Churchill in force and vigour as an orator; and in a speech delivered in Manchester he made an eloquent appeal to Liberals to join with Conservatives in forming a new political party, which he named 'Unionist,' to combine all that is best of the Tory, the Whig, and the Liberal.

In the interval of suspense which preceded Mr. Gladstone's declaration as to his Irish scheme, there was no ambiguity in the utterances of the Whig leaders, and he was made perfectly aware that if his Bill would confer a practically independent legislature on Ireland, he must prepare for opposition not only from them and the Tories, but also from Mr. Chamberlain and Mr. Trevelyan, his colleagues in the Cabinet. In March it was announced that they had resigned.

On April 8, 1886, Mr. Gladstone moved his great and long-expected measure. The desire to hear the statement of the Premier was intense, Nationalist members sitting up all night to secure their places. Never was there such a struggle on the part of members to obtain seats. Chairs were set on the floor of the House, by which means seventy or eighty additional seats were provided. The galleries, the nooks—in short, every foot of standing ground was crowded with chairs. Language fails to do justice to the intense excitement of the hour, or to note the competition for every seat in the Strangers' Gallery; the scramble of the Lords, too, for room in places assigned to them, the ovation rapturously afforded by his followers to the hero of the hour, the physical and mental efforts of the orator for more than two hours, the rapt attention, diversified by bursts of cheers from one side and ironical exclamations from the other, and the vociferous applause at the close, are things never to be forgotten in the history of our Parliamentary annals. The speech with which he wound up the debate on the first reading in April was wonderfully fine. 'He raised,' writes Sir R. Temple, 'the drooping spirits of his followers; he held his head aloft; and in his wrath against the dissentient Liberals he seemed to stand higher by inches than his ordinary stature.' His next effort, in unfolding his scheme for buying out the Irish landlords, was not so successful. After Mr. Chamberlain's attack on it, he is described as having left the House apparently in high dudgeon. The second reading of the Home Rule Bill was moved by Mr. Gladstone amidst cheers from the Nationalist members alone. The debate was animated and prolonged. On the closing night Mr. Gladstone rose at midnight to deliver his fourth speech on the Bill. 'For the last twenty minutes or so,' writes Sir R. Temple, 'I have never heard such oratory anywhere from any man; indeed, he poured his very soul into it.' But all in vain. The Ayes were 311, the Noes 341. Parliament was dissolved, and in the General Election Home Rule was smitten, as far as England was concerned, hip and thigh. Lord Salisbury was Premier, Mr. Goschen joined the Unionist party; and Mr. Chamberlain suggested the Round Table Conference to fill up the Liberal ranks, to which Mr. Gladstone heartily consented, but which came to nothing after all.

The chief event of this short session was a Tenant Relief Bill, introduced by Mr. Parnell, providing for the suspension of the ejectment of any defaulting tenant who should pay half his rent and half his arrears. Let us add, this session was memorable as the most trying one that had ever taken place, from the acrimony of its debates and the late hours of its sittings. However, Mr. Gladstone had got back Sir George Trevelyan and three or four small men besides. Meanwhile, the Government had to wince under the loss of several seats at by-elections. At Southampton, the Unionist majority of 342 had been turned into a Gladstonian one of 885; and the Ayr Burghs followed suit, by replacing a Unionist, whose majority had been at the General Election 1,175, by a Gladstonian whom they preferred to the extent of 53 votes to the Hon. Evelyn Ashley. It was not till Christmas Eve that Parliament adjourned. Government met Parliament the next year under great discouragement. Before the debate on the Queen's Speech was begun, Sir William Harcourt raised the question of privilege, of which he maintained a breach had been committed against the House by Tories in the matter of the charges against the Irish members; and the diminished majority by which his motion was rejected—58—testified to the loss of prestige by the Government, as a consequence of their supposed connection with a case bolstered up by the forgeries of the Irish informer Pigott. On the second reading of the Local Taxation Bill, Mr. Caine moved an amendment refusing assent to any proposal to extinguish licenses by means of public money. Mr. Gladstone, in supporting it, defended himself from the charge of having violated pledges given to his Midlothian electors, declared that since those pledges had been given 'the law had been cleared and settled in a manner not only unfavourable to the doctrine of vested interests, but likewise to the doctrine of permanent interest, on the part of a publican in an annual license.' However, Mr. Gladstone spoke in vain.

Mr. Justin McCarthy, in his 'Life of Mr. Gladstone,' seems to show the gradual development of Mr. Gladstone's conversion to Home Rule. This was not at all the sudden change that shallow satirists imagined. His conviction was gradually borne in upon him by the close study of Ireland imposed upon him as a preparation for his Church and Land legislation. He hesitated long, because Ireland had never sent a majority of Nationalists to Parliament. On this subject Mr. McCarthy's recollection of a conversation with the great chief in the division lobby is very interesting: 'He said to me in a somewhat emphatic tone that he could not understand why a mere handful of Irish members, such as my immediate colleagues were, should call themselves par excellence the Irish Nationalist Party, while a much larger number of Irish representatives, elected just as we were, kept always assuring him that the Irish people had no manner of sympathy with us or with our Home Rule scheme. "How am I to know?" he asked me. "These men far outnumber you and your friends, and they are as fairly elected as you are." I said to him: "Mr. Gladstone, give us a popular franchise in Ireland, and we will soon let you know whether we represent the Irish people or whether we do not." At the election of 1885 they did let him know, by returning 85 Nationalists out of 103 members for Ireland. This settled the question in Mr. Gladstone's mind.

When a serious calamity occurred to the Irish party by reason of the action brought against Mr. Parnell by Captain O'Shea for adultery with his wife, Mr. Gladstone was compelled to take notice of the matter. The English Nonconformists and Scotch Presbyterians made known to him their determination not to work for Home Rule so long as Mr. Parnell remained at the head of the Irish party. Accordingly, Mr. Gladstone wrote to Mr. John Morley: 'I thought it necessary, reviewing arrangements for the commencement of the present session, to acquaint Mr. McCarthy with the conclusion at which I have arrived, after using all the means of reflection and observation in my power. It was this, that, notwithstanding the splendid services rendered by Mr. Parnell to his country, his continuance at the present moment in the leadership would be productive of consequences disastrous in the highest degree to the cause of Ireland.'

This led to serious charges of bad faith made against Mr. Gladstone by Mr. Parnell. 'No single suggestion was offered by me,' wrote Mr. Gladstone in reply, 'as formal, or as unanimous, or final. It was a statement, perfectly free and without prejudice, of points in which either I myself or such of my colleagues as I had been able to consult inclined generally to believe that the plan for Home Rule in Ireland might be improved, and as to which I was desirous to learn whether they raised any serious objection in the mind of Mr. Parnell.'

In February, 1891, Mr. Gladstone moved the second reading of a Bill which he had introduced to remove the disabilities which prevented Roman Catholics from holding the appointment of Lord Chancellor and Viceroy of Ireland. The Bill was rejected by a majority of forty-seven. After this he almost entirely disappears from the Parliament he had done so much to illustrate and adorn. Never before has any statesman filled so large a space in public life, or secured so enormous a popularity. At times, even after 1892, there was talk of his returning to Parliament as leader, to head his followers, who were as sheep having no shepherd. But failing strength and advancing years led him to retire from Parliament altogether, and fainter grew his voice, and less frequent his utterances. Amongst the latest was his message to his party in 1898, to stick to Lord Rosebery and to attack the House of Lords. To the last the Nonconformists of England and Scotland, in spite of his High Church views, stuck to Mr. Gladstone. Largely had he been deserted by his old followers all over the country, who had cheered Mr. Gladstone when he indignantly told the leaders of the Irish party that their steps were dogged with crime; who had done their best to give him a majority that would render him, as he intimated, independent of the

Irish vote, but who failed to understand how, after such declarations, Mr. Gladstone could spring on them a Home Rule Bill, which they were not prepared to support. But none of these things affected the Nonconformist Conscience. In May, 1888, Mr. Gladstone received an address at the Memorial Hall in Farringdon Street, in favour of his Irish policy, signed by 3,370 Nonconformist ministers. To the address, which was read by the Rev. J. Guinness Rogers, Mr. Gladstone replied: 'I accept with gratitude, as well as pleasure, the address which has been presented to me, and I rejoice again to meet you within walls which, although no great number of years have passed away since their erection, have already become historic, and which are associated in my mind, and in the minds of many, with honourable struggles, sometimes under circumstances of depression, sometimes under circumstances of promise, but always leading us forward, whatever have been the phenomena of the moment, along the path of truth and justice. I am very thankful to those who have signed the address for the courageous manner in which they have not scrupled to associate their political action and intention with the principles and motives of their holy religion.'

Not long after came the end of Mr. Gladstone's marvellous Parliamentary career. The originative power, masterful vigour, and fiery energy which still characterized Mr. Gladstone after passing his eightieth year were so extraordinary that his followers almost regarded him as immortal. At any rate, men of forty and fifty hardly expected to have to look for another leader in their lifetime. But, nevertheless, the time came for his retirement—came suddenly, and without apparent cause. There were rumours, but there was nothing certain, and his last Parliamentary words, in grave condemnation of the changes made by the Lords in the Local Government Bill, were spoken in March, 1894. The description of the scene is one of the most effective passages in Mr. McCarthy's book:

'Some of us, of course, were in the secret, or at least were vaguely forewarned of what we had to expect. Shortly after Mr. Gladstone sat down I met Mr. John Morley in one of the lobbies. "Is that, then," I asked, "the very last speech?" "The very last," was his reply. "I don't believe one quarter of the men in the House understand it so," I said. "No," he replied, "but it is so, all the same." Mr. McCarthy continues: "No other man, not Mr. Gladstone, would probably on such an occasion have made it plain that he was giving his final farewell to the assembly which he had charmed and over which he had dominated by his eloquence for so many years. Lord Chatham certainly would not have allowed himself to pass out of public life without conveying to all men the idea that he spoke in Parliament for the last time. But Mr. Gladstone, with all his magnificent rhetorical gift, and with all his artistic instinct, had no thought of getting up a scene. . . . In the theatric sense I should describe his last speech as a dramatic failure. Numbers of men lounged out of the House when the speech was over, not having the least idea that they were never again to hear his voice in Parliamentary debate. Yet I for one do not regret that Mr. Gladstone thus took his leave of political life. I am not sorry that there were no fireworks; that there was no tableau; that there was no such dramatic fall of the curtain. The orator during his closing speech was inspired by one subject, and was not thinking of himself. A single sentence interjected in the course of the speech would have told every one of his hearers what was coming, and would have led to a demonstration such as was probably never before known in the House of Commons. It did not suit Mr. Gladstone's tastes or inclinations to lead up to any such demonstration, and therefore, while he warned the House of Commons as to its duties and its responsibilities, he said not a word about himself and about his action in the future. Parliamentary history lost something, no doubt, by the manner of his exhortation, but I think the character of the man will be regarded as all the greater because at so supreme a moment he forgot that the greatest Parliamentary career of the Victorian era had come at last to its close.'

About this time Mr. W. H. Smith, the 'Old Mortality' of Punch, writes: 'Gladstone is more kindly in his personal relations than I have ever known him, but he is physically much weaker, and the least exertion knocks him up.' Yet Mr. Gladstone long outlived his amiable critic. When in March Mr. W. H. Smith moved the adoption of the report of the Parnell Commission, Mr. Gladstone moved an amendment, and for two hours poured forth a stream of eloquence, writes Sir R. Temple, like molten and liquid gold from the furnace, with intonation and gesticulation quite marvellous for a man of his advanced age; but his amendment was rejected. In the debate on the Welsh Church he spoke for Disestablishment, contending that when he argued for the Establishment the political forces were for it, but now they were against it. In the next year Mr. Gladstone made a speech in favour of peasant proprietorship, and on the advantages of small tenures of land, as on the Continent. He also opposed a grant for a railway near Zanzibar. In a broad-minded and judicious manner he supported the Government Bill for developing legislative measures in India, and for giving the natives increased electoral rights. He also supported the Clergy Discipline (Immorality) Bill in terms, says Sir R. Temple, of noble generosity towards the organization of the Church, yet in language of courteous respect towards Nonconformists.

In the Parliament ruled over by Mr. Smith, Mr. Gladstone—'now seventy-six years,' writes Mr. Russell—entered on an extraordinary course of physical and intellectual efforts with voice and pen, 'in Parliament and on the platform,' on behalf of his favourite scheme of Irish Home Rule. In 1888 Mr. Neill O'Daunt writes: 'Mr. Gladstone has been justly and ably denouncing the Union in the Westminster Review and other periodicals. He has given many unanswerable arguments against it. He might add, however, that if you want to appreciate the evils of the Union, look at me, W. E. G. When Ireland lay crushed and prostrate beneath the miseries of a seven years' famine, when multitudes had perished by starvation, and when all who could obtain the passage-money fled to America, I, W. E. G., secured that propitious moment to give a spur to the exodus by adding 52 per cent. to the taxation of Ireland, and pleaded the terms of the Union as my justification for inflicting this scourge on the suffering people.'

It is characteristic of Mr. Gladstone's loyalty that when engaged in celebrating his golden wedding, he found time to attend the House of Commons and deliver a speech in support of the Royal Grants.

Mr. Gladstone had left Parliament, had passed away from public life. Fight was in him, nevertheless, to the last. When in the winter of 1898 he started for the South of France, according to newspaper reports, he advised his followers to continue the attack on the House of

Lords; and when the Irish celebrated St. Patrick's Day in March in London, he wrote to them, advising union if they would gain the day. I prefer, however, and I think many will agree with me, to think of the aged and illustrious man as he was leaving Bournemouth for Hawarden in March of the same year, putting his head out of the window, and saying to the crowd who had come to see him off: 'God bless you all, and the land you love!'

CHAPTER XII. MR. GLADSTONE'S SPEECHES.

In 1892 appeared part of what was to be a ten-volume edition of Mr. Gladstone's speeches, edited by Mr. William Hutton, librarian, National Liberal Club, and R. J. Cowen, of the Inner Temple, barrister-at-law. The work is a labour of love on the part of the two editors, and Mr. Gladstone himself contributes a modest preface. He has seen such passages as seemed to require revision, and he testifies to their correctness. In some instances the editors have made verbal amendments where it was apparent that the text was misreported. They have also added brief notes, just sufficient to recall the circumstances under which the speeches were delivered. It is in his perorations that Mr. Gladstone rises to his loftiest rhetoric, as is seen in the one delivered in his great Birmingham speech of 1885 on Ireland's new weapons: 'Ah, gentlemen, may I tell you with what weapons Ireland is fighting this battle? She is not fighting it with the weapons of menace, with a threat of separation, with Fenian outbreaks, with the extension of secret societies. Happily those ideas have passed away into a distance undefined. She is fighting the contest with the weapons of confidence and affection—of confidence in the powerful party by whose irrevocable decision she is supported, and of affection towards the people of England. May I tell you one incident, that will not occupy two minutes, in proof of what I say? In the county, I think, of Limerick, not very many days ago, an Englishman was addressing a crowd of Irish Nationalists on the subject of Home Rule. His carriage or his train, whichever it was, was just going to depart. Someone cried out, "God save Ireland!" and there was a loud burst of cheering. The train started, the cheering subsided. Another voice from the crowd was raised, and shouted, "And God save England!" and there were cheers louder still, such in the language of Shakespeare that

These cheers were the genuine expression of the sentiment of the country. They, our opponents, teach you to rely on the use of this deserted and enfeebled and superannuated weapon of coercion. We teach you to rely upon Irish affection and goodwill. We teach you not to speculate on the formation of that sentiment. We show you that it is formed already; it is in full force; it is ready to burst forth from every Irish heart and through every Irish voice. We only beseech you, by resolute adherence to that policy you have adopted, to foster, to cherish, to consolidate that sentiment, and so to act that in space it shall spread from the north of Ireland to the south, and from the west of Ireland to the east; and in time it shall extend and endure from the present date until the last of the years and the last of the centuries that may still be reserved in the counsels of Providence to work out the destinies of mankind.'

Perhaps more of our readers will agree with Mr. Gladstone's eulogy of books in opening a working men's library in Saltney:

'And now I commend you again to your books. Books are delightful society. If you go into a room and find it full of books—and without even taking them down from their shelves—they seem to speak to you, to bid you welcome. They seem to tell you that they have got something inside their covers that will be good for you, and that they are willing and desirous to impart to you. Value them much. Endeavour to turn them to good account, and pray recollect this, that the education of the mind is not merely a stowage of goods in the mind. The mind of man, some people seem to think, is a storehouse that should be filled with a quantity of useful commodities which may be taken out like packets from a shop, and delivered and distributed according to the occasions of life. I will not say that this is not true as far as it goes; but it goes a very little way, for commodities may be taken in and commodities may be given out, but the warehouse remains just the same as it was before, or probably a little worse. That ought not to be the case with a man's mind. No doubt you are to cull knowledge that is useful for the temporal purpose of life, but never forget that the purpose for which a man lives is the improvement of the man himself, so that he may go out of this world having, in his great sphere or his small one, done some little good to his fellow-creatures, and laboured a little to diminish the sin and the sorrow that are in the world. For his own growth and development a man should seek to acquire, to his full capacity, useful knowledge, in order to deal it out again according to the supreme purposes of education. I remember just now I said that, outside of science, the chance for a labouring man to acquire knowledge was comparatively very little, unless he acquire it through observation. The poet Gray describes the condition of the rustics of the village in these words:

We have witnessed an improvement upon that state of things. Knowledge has now begun to unroll her ample page, and chill Penury does not now so universally repress. Let that improvement itself be improved upon, not necessarily by grand, imposing designs, but by each of us according to his means, with the sedulous endeavour to do our duty to our neighbour and our service to our country. Let me express the fervent hope that this literary institute may thrive, and may largely and continuously contribute to the prosperity of Saltney and the happiness of its people.'

In the Dundee address on 'Art and Industry,' delivered on October 29, 1890, Mr. Gladstone half playfully, half seriously, denounced the vagaries of fashion:

'Now, shall I shock you if I tell you what perhaps is partly only a personal opinion of my own? The study of beauty has several very formidable enemies. One of them, of course, is haste in production, carelessness in production. Sometimes the desire for cheapness makes people think you cannot have cheapness and beauty together. But the particular enemy which I think is one of the most formidable of all to the true comprehension and true pursuit of beauty is that thing which is known under the name of fashion. That may seem strange to the young gentlemen who want to be smart in their dress. I will not speak of young ladies. To them I have no doubt it will sound as if I was using language certainly rash, and perhaps almost profane. What is fashion? Gentlemen and ladies, if the ladies have anything to do with it—I won't say whether it is so or not—what is fashion? Fashion of dress is perpetual change. Wherever there is perpetual change, if it is to be justifiable or if it is to be useful, there ought to be perpetual progress. But fashion is not perpetual progress; fashion is a zigzag. Fashion is a wheel which whirls round and round, and by-and-by, after a fashion has been left, after it has been discarded, if you have only a little patience to wait long enough, you will find you will go back to it. Ladies and gentlemen, you are young and I am old; I have seen this wheel of fashion going round and round, always puzzling you, like a firework wheel, but always landing in a total negation of progress, and with a strong tendency to the substitution of mere caprice and mere display for the true pursuit of beauty.'

In 1894 appeared another volume. Nominally it was the ninth volume, but the order of sequence is apparently to be from last to first. The new volume is one of the most important of the series, since it contains the great speech on introducing the first Home Rule Bill, and seventeen speeches of later date, mainly upon Home Rule. Some of these speeches present the great Parliamentary orator at his very highest—broad in sweep, dexterous in sword-play, flashing with wit, pellucid in expression, driving home his case with passionate appeal and a rush of ingenious argument. Whether we agree with him or not, it is impossible, even in cold print, not to admire the overpowering ability of the 'old Parliamentary hand.' Here is the peroration of the first great speech on introducing the first Home Rule Bill:

'However this may be, we are sensible that we have taken an important decision—our choice has been made. It has not been made without thought; it has been made in the full knowledge that trial and difficulty may confront us on our path. We have no right to say that Ireland through her constitutionally-chosen representatives will accept the plan I offer. Whether it will be so I do not know—I have no title to assume it—but if Ireland does not cheerfully accept it, it is impossible for us to attempt to force upon her what is intended to be a boon; nor can we possibly press England and Scotland to accord to Ireland what she does not heartily welcome and embrace. There are difficulties, but I rely upon the patriotism and sagacity of this House; I rely on the effects of free and full discussion; and I rely more than all upon the just and generous sentiments of the two British nations. Looking forward, I ask the House to assist us in the work which we have undertaken, and to believe that no trivial motive can have driven us to it—to assist us in this work which we believe will restore Parliament to its dignity, and legislation to its free and unimpeded course. I ask you to stay that waste of public treasure which is involved in the present system of government and legislation in Ireland; and which is not a waste only, but which demoralizes while it exhausts. I ask you to show to Europe and to America that we, too, can face political problems which America twenty years ago faced, and which many countries in Europe have been called upon to face, and have not feared to deal with. I ask that in our own case we should practise with firm and fearless hand what we have so often preached—the doctrine which we have so often inculcated upon others—namely, that the concession of local self-government is not the way to sap or impair, but the way to strengthen and consolidate, unity. I ask that we should learn to rely less upon merely written stipulations, and more upon those better stipulations which are written on the heart and mind of man. I ask that we should apply to Ireland that happy experience which we have gained in England and in Scotland, where the course of generations has now taught us, not as a dream or a theory, but as practice and as life, that the best and surest foundation we can find to build upon is the foundation afforded by the affections, the convictions, and the will of the nation; and it is thus, by the decree of the Almighty, that we may be enabled to secure at once the social peace, the fame, the power, and the permanence of the empire.'

In another style, but very characteristic, I quote from the speech delivered by Mr. Gladstone at

Hawarden in the Jubilee year, reviewing the reign of the Queen:

'Now, I have said quite enough for this occasion, and I think enough to justify me in reminding you that although a jubilee may be regarded as an affair of form and ceremony, there is a great deal more than form and ceremony in this Jubilee. It invites us and compels us to cast our thoughts backward over that long series of years with which we are almost all of us familiar, and it imposes upon us the duty of deep thankfulness to the Almighty, who in these late days, when our history is so long, and when some might have thought that our nation and our constitution had grown old, has given us as a people a renovated youth; who has inspired us with renewed activity and with buoyant hope; who has conducted us thus far upon the road to improvement and advancement in the pursuit, not of false, but of true human happiness; who has made the laws of this country no longer odious, no longer suspected, but dear to the people at large, and who has thereby encouraged us—I will not say much of encouragement to men of my age, whose life is in the past more than in the future—it has encouraged all those who are grown up or coming on, who are in the first glow of youth or in the prime and vigour of manhood, to persevere and endeavour to make the coming years, if they can, not worse, but better than those which have gone by. I beseech you, if you owe the debt of gratitude to the Queen for that which I have described, for her hearty concurrence in the work of public progress and improvement, for the admirable public example which her life has uniformly set, for her thorough comprehension of the true conditions of the great covenant between the throne and the people—if you owe her a debt of gratitude for these, may I say to you: Try to acknowledge that debt by remembering her in your prayers. Depend upon it that when St. Paul enjoined that prayers should be made for all men, and gave the commanding and the leading place to prayers for kings and all in authority, St. Paul spoke the language not only of religion, but of the most profound social justice and human common-sense. Do not imagine that because in this world some live in greater splendour and greater enjoyment than others, they therefore live free of temptation, so as not to need the prayers of their fellow-Christians. Depend upon it, the higher placed one is in society, the greater are his difficulties, and the more subtle the temptations that surround his path, and that which is true as we rise from rank to rank is not least of all, but most of all, true when we come to the elevated and august position of the Sovereign, who, as a sovereign, more than any one among her subjects, needs the support which the prayers and the intercessions of her subjects offered for her to her Saviour can afford. Forgive me for entreating you not to forget that duty; not to forget that simple mode at the command of all, in which everyone who thinks the Queen has nobly done her duty to them may perform a great and beneficial duty to her and for her.'

We give one other extract from a speech at Swansea in 1887—'The Union of Hearts':

'No difference connected with this question ought for a moment to impede our steady march upon the path on which we are entered—the path which leads us to a happy consummation of a just and politic arrangement between the two nations. I have reminded you of the objects which the arrangement contemplated—objects the dearest of which can endear them to the hearts of men, the greatness of the empire, the solidity of the empire, the true cohesion of the empire, the happiness of the people, the union of classes, the establishment of social order, the rule of law by moral as well as by physical force in one of the great divisions of the country, and finally the restoration of the honour and character of the country, so grievously compromised by this painful subject. These are the objects which make our present arduous labours worth persevering in and make us determined to pursue them. There was on one of the banners we saw to-day a phrase that I referred to in addressing our friends outside, and which made a deep impression upon me—"The union of hearts, not manacles." What is our union with Ireland now? It is the union of manacles, and not of hearts. It is a force that attaches Ireland to us. What said Mr. Bright? If Ireland were towed out 2,000 miles into the Atlantic your relations with Ireland would be at an end. We want to substitute for that union of force the union of hearts. We want that Ireland shall be united to England as Wales is united to England, as Scotland is united to England, not that they should be dead to their own national interests and concerns, but that they should desire to pursue them and promote them as measures of a firmly united and compacted empire. We have a state of things in Ireland by which, if we seize and do not lose the golden opportunity, this same union may be gained. While Ireland, in consonance with her traditions and in consequence of those physical circumstances by which she is divided from us by the Channel, desires the management of her own concerns, she is happily disposed to union with us, and to be at one with us in everything that concerns the greatness of the empire; but if this golden opportunity be lost we know not when it will return. The rule is that lost opportunities do not return, or, if they return, they return only after long intervals and after heavy damages have been paid for the original neglect. God grant that these mischiefs may be avoided—at any rate, with regard to the subject that is now before us.'

A remarkable illustration of Mr. Gladstone's many-sidedness is to be found in the fact that on one occasion he went to dine with the poor at St. Pancras Workhouse in 1879, with 600 of the aged inmates, at a dinner given by Mr. E. Skerries, one of the guardians. In the course of his speech Mr. Gladstone said: 'My life presents to me a great variety of scenes and occasions; but among all these scenes and occasions I tell you, with unfeigned sincerity, I have not witnessed one for a long time that has filled me with heartier or tenderer pleasure than to be a guest at the present assembly. I likewise desired, I am well aware, in a slight manner to take an opportunity which does not often occur to me of testifying, as far as I can, my interest in your lot. In this great establishment of which you are inmates it is not possible, consistently with the interests of the community, to give many indulgences by rule and under system, which I am convinced many of those who govern you would desire to give if they felt it could be done with safety. It is not because the giving or receiving of such indulgences would be mischievous or dangerous to yourselves; it is the effect, which I am quite sure you can well appreciate, which would be produced upon the community at large, if these establishments, which are maintained out of the labour of the community and at its charge, were made establishments of luxurious living. It is necessary that the independent labourer of the country should not be solicited and tempted to forego his duty to his wife and children and the community by thinking that he could do better for himself by making himself a charge on that community. There is no more subtle poison that could be infused into the community than a system of that kind. We were in danger of it some fifty or sixty years ago, but the spirit and courage of the Parliament of 1834 and the Government of that day introduced a sounder system, and matters are here regulated with what I believe and trust is—and I believe you would be able to echo what I say—with firmness and kindness.'

When the charges against Mr. Parnell and his friends were made in the House of Commons, Mr. Gladstone was strongly against their vindication of themselves in a court of law—on the first ground, on the plea of the law's delay, and, secondly, from the character of our judges. He blamed Lord Randolph Churchill for speaking in their favour. He entirely differed from that noble lord as to the judges. He believed all judges now on the bench could be trusted perfectly. But there was one judge now upon the bench who came down from the bench to take a part in regard to the great Irish Question more violent than had been taken by any layman he could remember. If one of the gentlemen sitting below the gangway said it was excusable in him to feel some mistrust in such a case, though he (Mr. Gladstone) should not feel mistrust himself, he could understand that mistrust. Was it so certain a verdict would be got? As to the certainty of getting verdicts against newspapers in cases where a public man attempted to restrain the liberty of newspaper comment on his own conduct, he might mention that thirty years ago he had the honour to serve Her Majesty as High Commissioner of the Ionian Islands. The people of the Ionian Islands had little or nothing to complain of as to practical grievances, but they were possessed with an intense sentiment of nationality. That sentiment determined them to be content with nothing except union with their own blood and race, and that sentiment was treated by a portion of the press of this country, and especially by a portion of the Metropolitan press, with unmeasured and bitter contempt. It was said: 'Who are these miserable Ionians that desire to join themselves to an equally miserable set of people in Greece, instead of welcoming the glory of being attached to a great empire?' The Times said, in effect: 'The Ionian Assembly has been committing treason, and the Queen's Commissioner has been aiding them to commit that treason.' He determined to prosecute the Times. He took the best advice from legal friends of weight and character, and every one of those gentlemen said: 'Don't dream of it. You cannot get a verdict.' He would have gone into court without one particular prejudice against him, but in this case there was in the minds of a portion of the public a gross and cruel prejudice. His legal advisers protested so positively against any such trial that he had to acquiesce in that gross and monstrous charge. Juries had a just and proper prejudice in favour of the liberty of the press, and if he himself were a juror it would take very much indeed to make him give a verdict in restraint of the liberty of the press. He could not think they were entitled to condemn in the slightest degree the hon. member for East Mayo, if he declined to commit himself to the mercy or the chance of a court of law.

As another proof of Mr. Gladstone's versatility, let us notice a speech delivered at the Hawarden Flower Show on fruit and vegetable culture, in which he dwelt on the importance of garden cultivation. He commenced by remarking that that was a time when leading people had to consider more seriously than they were accustomed to do in times of prosperity how they could better their position, and struggle with the vicissitudes of time and climate more effectually than on former occasions they had been able to do. 'I believe,' said Mr. Gladstone, 'that one of the modes in which the cultivators of the soil in this country—I will draw no distinction at present between small and large—may improve their position is by paying a greater attention to what is called garden and spade cultivation. Perhaps it will surprise you if I tell you what is the value of the fruit and vegetables imported into this country from abroad. Now, of dried fruits there are imported into this country a value of about £2,346,000. I don't speak so much of those, because a large proportion consists of products, such as currants, figs, and raisins, that are not adapted to the latitude of this country; but I find that a vast quantity is imported of raw fruit, such as apples, pears, stone-fruit, and the like. No less than £1,704,000 worth of raw fruit is generally imported into this country. Then, when I come to vegetables, a still larger proportion is imported. There are £414,000 worth of onions imported, but, I take it, there is no better country for the growth of onions than this country. There were, taking potatoes and other kinds of vegetables, about £5,000,000 imported. I should like to see this fruit and these vegetables grown at home.' Mr. Gladstone then went on to show how lucrative was the growing of vegetables. 'There was a natural taste on the part of the people to cottage garden cultivation, and a vast deal of profitable industry might be set in motion by the extension of this cottage gardening, and by the introduction of the spade cultivation where it was found suitable, even upon larger masses of land than were at the command of cottagers.'

At a breakfast in 1887, given by Dr. Parker, at which a large number of Nonconformist ministers were present, in the course of his speech Mr. Gladstone said: 'I have no difficulty whatever in referring to the language which I myself and others have used in respect to the Irish party about six years ago, and in bringing that language into comparison with what I have said of them within the last few weeks. Six years ago it was our conviction that the leaders of the Irish party were engaged in operations which, although they might have considered them to be justified and called for by the circumstances of the country, we thought were of a blamable and dangerous, and even ruinous character. I did say at that time that the footsteps of what was called the Land League were, in my opinion, dogged with crime—that where the Land League went, crime followed it. I did say at that time, when, as we believed, there was a general movement against the payment of rates and fulfilling of contracts as a whole—I did say at that time that it was a question of proceeding through rapine to dismemberment. Those were very grave words to use. They may have been warranted, or they may have been unwarranted; they may have been exaggerated, or they may have been justified by the circumstances of the case, but I believed them, and they were spoken with sincerity. I am bound to say this, that I am not prepared to say at this moment that they were without force and truth. Grave charges were made at that time by the Nationalist party against us. Some of those charges I can now see to have been true, and I see that that is the case not for the first time. I see that some of the measures which we proposed, especially the measure for the suspension of the Habeas Corpus Act, were unhappy and mischievous measures; but we spoke according to the circumstances that were before us. It is quite true that we were aware then, as now, that enormous allowances were to be made for men acting in Ireland under the difficulties of their position, and with the smarting and painful recollection of their past history; but we spoke the truth then, and we speak the truth now. The other day, following the steps of Lord Spencer, I stated in public that there was not, so far as I knew, and that there never had been, any reason for charging upon Mr. Parnell and the members of the Irish party complicity with crime. That is perfectly true; and it is what I would have said six years ago. I believed then that their language was dangerous, and that their plans were questionable, that they had a tendency to the production of crime; but that is a thing totally different from complicity with crime.'

CHAPTER XIII. MR. GLADSTONE'S PUBLICATIONS.

When George III. was King, two of his servants, as retired Ministers, met one another at Bath. Said one of them, Lord Mendip, to the other, Lord Camden, 'I hope you are well and in the enjoyment of a happy old age.' Lord Camden replied in a querulous tone: 'Happy! How can a man be happy who has survived all his passions and enjoyments?' 'Oh, my dear lord,' was the reply of his old antagonist, 'do not talk so; while God is pleased to enable me to read my Homer and my Bible, I cannot but be thankful and happy.' It is easy to imagine Mr. Gladstone making a similar reply. His love of Homer is only equalled by his love of the Bible. Porson used to say of Bishop Pearson that, if he had not muddled his head with theology, he would have been a first-class critic in Greek. Mr. Gladstone, as we have seen, has had a good deal to do with theology, but that he has not muddled his brains with it is clear, not merely from his active life as a statesman, but from the perusal of the many valuable works he has written on Homer, and his life and time and work. The subject seems to have endless attractions for him. Charles James Fox used to read Homer through every year. Mr. Gladstone displays a still greater enthusiasm. In this department of human inquiry he has been emphatically distinguished, and his works on Homer, to do them adequate justice, would require a volume by no means small to themselves. In 1838 his first great work on the subject appeared. It was entitled 'Studies of Homer and the Homeric Age,' and consisted of three large volumes. In 1869 he republished and rewrote a great part of the previous volumes in his 'Juventus Mundi: the Gods and Men of the Heroic Age.' 'I am anxious,' he writes, 'to commend to inquirers and readers generally conclusions from the Homeric poems which appear to me to be of great interest with reference to the general history of human culture, and in connection therewith with the Providential government of the world. But I am much more anxious to encourage and facilitate the access of educated persons to the actual contents of the text. The amount and variety of these contents have not been fully apparent. The delight received from the poems has possibly had some influence in disposing the generality of readers to rest satisfied with their enjoyment. The doubts cast upon their origin must have assisted in producing and fostering a vague instinctive indisposition to further laborious examination. The very splendour of the poems dazzles the eyes with whole sheets of lightning, and may almost give to analysis the character of vulgarity or impertinence.' In his preface Mr. Gladstone tells us that his ideas have been considerably modified in the ethnological and mythological portions of his inquiry. The chief source of modification in the former has been that a further prosecution of the subject with respect to the Phœnicians has brought out more clearly and fully what he had only ventured to suspect—a highly influential function in forming the Greek element. A fuller view of this element in its composition naturally aids in an important manner upon any estimate of Pelasgians and Hellenes respectively. This Phœnician influence reaches far into the sphere of mythology, and tends, as he thinks, greatly to clear the views we may reasonably take of that curious and interesting subject. The aim of this revised edition of his Homeric studies was to assist Homeric studies in our schools and Universities, and to convey a practical knowledge of the subject to persons who are not habitual students.

Few men have found time to appear in print so frequently as Mr. Gladstone. His latest publication bears the date of 1898; his earliest appeared in 1837. One of his great topics has been Homer. The old Greek poet ought to be, according to Mr. Gladstone, in everyone's hands. His latest work on the subject was the 'Landmarks of Homeric Study, together with an Essay on the Points of Contact between the Assyrian Tablets and the Homeric Text,' which appeared in 1890. Among the numberless solutions of the Homeric question since the days of Wolff, he still maintains the traditional view that there was but one Homer, that he wrote both poems, and that the poems themselves should be regarded as a historic whole. In Mr. Gladstone's view one of Homer's chief functions was to weld the diverse elements of the Hellenic nation into one. National unity necessarily involved religious unity, and so Mr. Gladstone goes on to propound the theory that Homer endeavoured to find a place in his heaven for all the gods that had been worshipped by the different races he was welding together, and that with this view he created a composite system of religion. It affords us matter for wonder, he says, as well as admiration, how Homer excluded from this new composite system the most degrading ingredients in which the religions around him abounded. Though forced to admit Aphrodite, he only admitted her to a lower place, and presented her in an unfavourable light. She is, in fact, only the Assyrian Ishtar, the Ashtoreth of the Hebrews and Phœnicians. He also elaborately contends that there was a good deal of morality among Homer's Greeks, far more than is generally supposed. The Politics of Homer form another chapter, and he finds high praise for the value the poet attached to personal freedom, and in the extraordinary power for those times he attached to the spoken word. Except in the concluding chapter on Assyrian Tablets and the Homeric Texts, Mr. Gladstone added little to what is to be found in one or other of his previous books.

In 1896 appeared 'The Impregnable Rock of Holy Scripture,' revised and enlarged from Good Words. The argument appears to be that in the science and history of the Holy Bible there may be detected a degree of accuracy plainly supernatural and miraculous. With great warmth he owns his desire to prevent his countrymen from relaxing their hold on the Bible, which Christendom regards as 'an inestimable treasure,' and thus bringing on themselves 'inexpressible calamity.' He adopts towards Hebrew specialists an attitude neither defiant nor abjectly submissive. The meaning of Hebrew words must, of course, be determined by Hebrew scholars; but he argues that we must not forget the risks to which specialists themselves are exposed. 'Among them,' he writes, 'as with other men, there may be fashions of the time and school, which Lord Bacon called idols of the market-place, and currents of prejudice below the surface, such as to detract somewhat from the authority which each inquirer may justly claim in his own field, and from their title to impose these conclusions upon mankind.' And so often has it already happened that the Bible was supposed to be submerged by some wave of opinion, which proved, after all, to be passing and ephemeral, that we may have confidence in its power of weathering storms. He holds that if, even for argument's sake, one concession were to be made to specialists of all they can be entitled to ask respecting the age, the authorship, the text of the books, he may still invite his readers to stand with him on the impregnable rock of Holy Scripture. Apart from all that science or criticism may say, he can still challenge men to accept the Scriptures on the moral and spiritual and historical ground of their character in themselves. In the course of his work he treats successively of the creation story as told in the first chapter of Genesis, of the Psalms, of the Mosaic legislation, of the Deluge, and of recent corroborations of Scripture from history and natural science.

In 1848 Mr. Gladstone wrote a Latin version of Toplady's hymn, 'Rock of Ages,' though it did not appear till 1861, when it was published in a volume of translations by himself and Lord Lyttelton, issued by them in memory of their marriage to two sisters. The following is the translation:

In 1863 Mr. Gladstone printed his translation of the first book of the 'Iliad.' He sent a copy to Lord Lyndhurst, then in his ninety-first year. The aged critic replied in the following letter. The accident to which it alludes was one which had happened some days before to Mr. Gladstone when riding in the Park:

Mr. Gladstone thought so highly of this criticism that he wrote back asking permission to print it in a contemplated preface to his translation. 'It is not,' he said, 'from a mere wish to parade you as my correspondent, though this wish may have its share. Your observation on my metre, which has great force, cuts, I think, deep into the matter—into the principles of Homeric translation. So pray let me have your permission.'

As an illustration of Mr. Gladstone's skill as a translator, let me add some verses from his version of the 'Hecuba' of Euripides, seven pages of which appeared in the Contemporary Review a few years since, though the translation was made in his Eton days:

In 1892 appeared 'An Academic Sketch' by the Right Hon. W. E. Gladstone, M.P., being the Romanes Lecture delivered in the Sheldon Theatre, Oxford. Whilst it did not detract from, it scarcely added to, Mr. Gladstone's reputation. It was, in fact, a speech somewhat of the after-dinner type. All the world knew that the Oxford of the past was a theme on which he could pleasantly dilate.

In 1894 there appeared from Mr. Gladstone's pen an article in the Nineteenth Century on the 'Atonement,' occasioned by the study of Mrs. Besant's 'Autobiography.' He says of her: 'Mrs. Besant passes from her earliest to her latest stage of thought as lightly as a swallow skims the surface of the lawn, and with just as little effort to ascertain what lies beneath it. Her several schemes of belief or non-belief appear to have been entertained one after another with the same undoubting confidence, until the junctures successively arrived for their not regretful, but rather contemptuous, rejection. They are nowhere based upon reasoning, but on the authority of Mrs. Besant.' The special proposition which Mr. Gladstone examines is one of four, the difficulties of which led Mrs. Besant to reject Christianity—the nature of the atonement of Christ. In dealing with this topic, Mr. Gladstone, after condemning the crude utterances of some theologians and preachers, by whom the New Testament doctrine has been travestied and misconceived, lays down what he conceives to be the true teaching. 'What is here enacted in the kingdom of grace only repeats a phenomenon with which we are perfectly familiar in the natural and social order of the world, where the good, at the expense of pain endured by them, procure benefits for the unworthy.'

In the same year appeared Mr. Gladstone's Horace. It was on the whole a failure. A critic writes: 'The uncouth diction, obscurity of expression of the rendering, are patent evidences of the translator's being ill at ease under the restraint of narrow bounds of rhyme and metre.' The same writer observes: 'Mr. Gladstone's translation of the Odes of Horace will escape oblivion. Historians will remember it as they remember the hexameters of Cicero, the verses with which Frederick the Great pestered Voltaire, and the daily poems Warren Hastings used to read at his breakfast-table.' An ingenious contributor to Blackwood, on the publication of the book, contributed a letter from 'Horace in the Shades,' intimating that he had nothing to do with the matter. It is to be questioned whether worse verses were ever written than the following in the 'Horace':

Again,

Or,

Thus is the death of Cleopatra recorded:

When 'Ecce Homo' appeared—a book which dear Lord Shaftesbury, Exeter Hall applauding, described as the worst book ever vomited out of the jaws of hell—Mr. Gladstone, in an article in Good Words, gave in his adherence to the book. He described the author as at once passing into the presence of Jesus of Nazareth, and then, without any foregone conclusion, either of submission or dissent, giving that heed to the acts and words of the unfriended teacher which the truest Jews did when those words were spoken and those acts done.

Mr. Gladstone found time, amid his preoccupations, to write a long article for the English Historical Review on the last portion of the 'Greville Memoirs,' chiefly justifying the action of the parties with which he was associated at the time of the 'death and obsequies of Protection,' in 1852, and during the Crimean War. Mr. Gladstone traverses Mr. Greville's statement that in 1852 the Peelites were indisposed to join the Whigs, under the delusive belief that they could form a Government of their own. He can say positively that, with the single exception of the Duke of Newcastle, none of the party entertained this belief. 'They knew that dichotomy, and not trichotomy, was for our times the law of the nation's life.' Their sympathies in regard to economy and peace lay rather with one of the Liberal wings than with the main body. In some cases they were divided between their Liberal opinions and their Conservative traditions and associations. For many a man to leave the party in which he was brought up is like the stroke of a sword dividing bone and marrow. But the intermediate position is essentially a false position, and nothing can long disguise its falseness. The right hon. gentleman confesses that he himself frankly stated to Lord Derby that the Peelites were a public nuisance, for while rapid migrations from camp to camp may be less creditable, slow ones not only are more painful, but are attended with protracted public inconvenience. The lessons of this political drama, he says—and the statement is significant at the present time—are of the present and the future. It entails a heavy responsibility to embark political parties in controversies certain to end in defeat where there is a silent sense of what is coming—a latent intention to accept defeat—and where the postponement of the final issue means only the enhancement of the price to be paid at the close. Mr. Gladstone deprecates the tone generally assumed in speaking of the Crimean War. He denies the assumptions that we drifted into that war; that the Cabinet of the day was in continual conflict with itself at the various stages of the negotiations; and that if it had adopted a bolder course at an earlier stage the Emperor Nicholas would have succumbed. The first of these assertions he characterizes as untrue, the second as ridiculous, and the third as speculative and highly improbable. Lord Clarendon did say that we drifted into war; but his meaning was simply that the time of war had not come, but the time of measures for averting it had expired; and Lord Clarendon, not less expressively than truly, said that, while the intermediate days were gliding by, we were drifting into war. 'But the fable is brazen-fronted, and, like Pope Joan, still holds her place.' As regards the Cabinet, Mr. Gladstone has witnessed much more sharp or warm argument in almost every other of the seven Cabinets to which he has had the honour to belong. In regard to the assumption that the war was not justifiable, he makes the 'inconvenient admission' that those who approved of the war at the time approved of it on very different grounds. Some favoured it as an Arthurian enterprise, the general defence of the weak against the strong; some because they had faith in the restorative energies of Turkey, if time were obtained by warding off the foe; some thought the power of Russia was exorbitant, and dangerous to Europe and to England. This last was the sentiment which most captivated the popular imagination. 'It was feeling, and not argument, that raised the Crimean War into popularity.' It is feeling, Mr. Gladstone thinks, which has plunged it into the abyss of odium. The war proceeded, as he conceives, upon a more just and noble idea expressed by Lord Russell when, on the outbreak of hostilities, he denounced the Emperor Nicholas as 'the wanton disturber of the peace of Europe.' The policy which led to the war was a European protest against the wrongdoing of a single State. His belief is that, compared with most wars, the war of 1854–56 will hold in history no dishonourable place. For its policy must be regarded à parte ante. He confesses, however, that the result of the war was exceedingly unsatisfactory.

The May number of the Nineteenth Century, 1887, contained an article by Mr. Gladstone reviewing the fifth and sixth volumes of Mr. Lecky's 'History of England in the Eighteenth Century.' Towards the conclusion of the article Mr. Gladstone quotes the following sentence:

'Mr. Lecky writes as follows: "We have seen a Minister going to the country on the promise that if he was returned to office he would abolish the principal direct tax paid by the class which was then predominant in the constituencies."'

This sentence refers, of course, to Mr. Gladstone's promise in his election address in 1874 to repeal the income tax. Mr. Gladstone replies that Mr. Lecky seems to be unaware that it is the practice of candidates for a seat in Parliament to announce to those whose votes they desire their views on political questions, either pending, proximate, or sometimes remote. He proceeds:

'The accusing sentence is inaccurately written. In January, 1874, the date to which it refers, there was no question of returning to office. I addressed a constituency as Minister, and in a double capacity as Chancellor of the Exchequer and as head of the Administration, proposed to repeal the income tax. But it is also untruly written. It is untrue that the payers of income tax were then the predominant class in the constituencies. In Ireland, the payers of income tax had ceased, since the ballot was introduced, to rule elections. In England and Scotland, a very large majority of members were returned by the towns. In the towns, then as now, household suffrage was in full force, and the voters were as a body more independent of the wealthy than are the rural population. The repeal of the income tax, whether proper or improper in itself, was not then a thing improper in respect of the persons to whom it was announced.

'It has been held by some that there should never be an appeal to the people by a Ministry on the subject of taxation. But why not? The rights of the people in respect to taxation are older, higher, clearer, than in respect to any other subject of government. Now, appeals on many such subjects have been properly made—on Reform in 1831; on the China War in 1857; on the Irish Church in 1868; on Home Rule in 1886; lastly, in 1852, by the Tories, whose creed Mr. Lecky appears in other matters to have adopted, on the finance proper to be proposed by Mr. Disraeli after, and in connection with, the repeal of the Corn Law.

'Undoubtedly, although right in principle, such appeals and promises are eminently liable to abuse. But there is one touchstone by which the peccant element in them may be at once detected. If the promise launches into the far future, it may straightway be condemned. If, on the other hand, it is one certain to be tested within a few weeks, the case is different. A Minister casually pitchforked, so to speak, into office, and living from hand to mouth, might be tempted to a desperate venture. But can Mr. Lecky suppose that the Ministry of 1868–74, which had outlived the ordinary term, and (may it be said?) had made its mark in history, would thus have gambled with false coin, and have sought to add so ignobly, and with such compromise of character, a respite almost infinitesimal to its duration?

'Was the engagement to the repeal of the income tax one either obligatory or proper in itself? Was the time well chosen? Was the proposer morally bound to the proposal? I will answer "Yes" to all these questions, and I will prove my affirmative, though my short recital will lead Mr. Lecky, if he reads it, into a field of contemporary history which it is quite plain that he has never traversed.'

In 1895 it was announced that Mr. Gladstone had written a book on 'The Psalter, according to the Prayer-book Version.' It was commenced by Mr. Gladstone many years before, but it was not till his retirement from office that he found time to finish it. He also compiled a Concordance, and added a series of notes on the Psalter. In the same year the address on the Armenian question, which was delivered by Mr. Gladstone at Chester, was republished in pamphlet form by Mr. Fisher Unwin.

I may not omit to refer to Mr. Gladstone's utterance on the first chapter of Genesis—that sublime exordium to the Bible—that its truth is in all respects as fresh to-day as it was in the hour of its first enunciation, and that it links the Church of Adam, Abraham, and Moses in living fellowship and unity to the Church of to-day.

In 1894 Mr. Gladstone republished certain papers, which had already appeared in various periodicals, under the title of 'Studies Subsidiary to the Works of Bishop Butler.' He ridicules critics such as Matthew Arnold, who held that the 'Analogy' is dead, with the eighteenth-century Deism it opposed. He labours to show that it is as applicable to the religious problems of to-day as to those a hundred years old. The 'Analogy,' he holds, is one of the finest of intellectual disciplines. In the study of Butler's works the student finds himself in an intellectual palæstra, where his best exertions are required thoroughly to grapple with his teacher. Mainly, education is a process of wrestling, and it is best to wrestle with the highest masters. The chapters on the Censors of Butler shows all the ex-Premier's skill at fence. On the subject of the Theology of Butler, Mr. Gladstone attributes his habit of drawing it straight from the Scriptures, with little reference to authorities, as due to his Nonconformist education. In reply to the charges that the 'Analogy' tended to Romanism, he asks for a single known case where the study of Butler had led to Rome. The chapter on the influence of Butler is of great interest. In his second part Mr. Gladstone is occupied largely with an elaborate discussion, on the lines laid down by Butler, on the future life, and the condition of man therein. He is especially severe on the Universalists. He regards a period of future discipline for imperfect natures, 'not without an admixture of salutary and accepted grace,' as in accord with both faith and reason. The remaining chapters on Determinism, Teleology, Miracle, and Probability are the toughest in the whole book, and are as hard to understand as Butler himself. On miracles Mr. Gladstone follows the orthodox lines.

Mr. Gladstone's latest utterances on the subject of Christianity appeared in 1895. He pleads for an eternity of punishment. His latest article on the subject appeared in the American Pictorial Bible. The following passage, in which he surveys the world, is worth reprinting: 'The Christian religion,' he says, 'is for mankind the greatest of all phenomena. It is the dominant religion of the inhabitants of this planet in at least two important respects. It commands the largest number of professing adherents. If we estimate the population of the globe at 1,400,000,000—and some would state it at a higher figure—between 400 and 500 of these, or one-third of the whole, are professing Christians; and at every point of the circuit the question is not one of losing ground, but of gaining it. The fallacy which accepted the vast population of China as Buddhists in the mass has been exploded, and it is plain that no other religion approaches the numerical strength of Christianity—doubtful, indeed, if there be any other which reaches one-half of it. The second of the particulars now under view is perhaps more important. Christianity is the religion in the command of whose professors is lodged a proportion of power far exceeding its superiority of numbers, and this power is both moral and material. In the area of controversy it can be said to have hardly an antagonist. Force, secular or physical, is accumulated in the hands of Christians in a proportion almost overwhelming, and the accumulation of influence is not less remarkable than that of force. This is not surprising, for all the elements of influence have their home within the Christian precinct. The art, the literature, the systematic industry, invention, and commerce—in one word, the forces of the world are almost wholly Christian. In Christendom alone there seems to be an inexhaustible energy of world-wide expansion.'

In conclusion, we give a couple of extracts from Mr. Gladstone's more recent articles of universal interest. In one he makes a noble contribution to the praise of books. 'Books are,' he says, 'the voices of the dead. They are a main instrument of communion with the vast human procession of the other world. They are the allies of the thought of men. They are in a certain sense at enmity with the world. Their work is, at least, in the two higher compartments of our threefold life. In a room well filled with them no one has felt or can feel solitary. Second to none, as friends to the individual, they are first and foremost among the compages, the bonds and rivets of the race.' But books want housing and arranging, and they are multiplying so rapidly that they threaten to get beyond all control. In an article in the Nineteenth Century, from which we quote the above, Mr. Gladstone, with a light-hearted relish of the subject it is pleasant to see, gives some of his ideas on the subject of arrangement.

Another extract will give us his ideas of the Jews. He thinks that the purport of the Old Testament can be best summed up in the words that it is a history of sin and redemption. After explaining that the narrative of the Fall is in accordance with the laws of a grand and comprehensive philosophy, and that the objections taken to it are the product of narrower and shallower modes of thought, he proceeds, passing by the story of the Deluge and the dispersion, to consider the selection of Abraham. 'Why,' he asks, 'were the Jews selected as the chosen people of God?' Not, he thinks, because of their moral superiority. He contrasts the Jewish ethics and those of the Greeks, considerably to the detriment of the former, and then sums up the matter as follows: 'Enough has perhaps been said to show that we cannot claim as a thing demonstrable a great moral superiority for the Hebrew line generally over the whole of the historically known contemporary races. I, nevertheless, cannot but believe that there was an interior circle, known to us by its fruits in the Psalter and the prophetic books, of morality and sanctity altogether superior to what was to be found elsewhere, and due rather to the pre-Mosaic than to the Mosaic religion of the race. But it remains to answer with reverence the question, Why, if not for a distinctly superior morality, nor as a full religious provision for the whole wants of man, why was the race chosen as a race to receive the promises, to guard the oracles, and to fulfil the hopes of the great Redemption?

'The answer may, I believe, be conveyed in moderate compass. The design of the Almighty, as we everywhere find, was to prepare the human race, by a varied and a prolonged education, for the arrival of the great Redemption. The immediate purposes of the Abrahamic selection may have been to appoint, for the task of preserving in the world the fundamental bases of religion, a race which possessed qualifications for that end decisively surpassing those of all other races. We may easily indicate two of these fundamental bases. The first was the belief in one God. The second was the knowledge that the race had departed from His laws—without which knowledge how should they welcome a Deliverer whose object it was to bring them back? It may be stated with confidence that among the dominant races of the world the belief in one God was speedily destroyed by polytheism, and the idea of sin faded gradually but utterly away. Is it audacious to say that what was wanted was a race so endowed with the qualities of masculine tenacity and persistency, as to hold over these all-important truths until that fulness of time when, by and with them, the complete design of the Almighty would be revealed to the world? A long experience of trials beyond all example has proved since the Advent how the Jews, in this one essential quality, have surpassed every other people upon earth. A marvellous and glorious experience has shown how among their ancestors before the Advent were kept alive and in full vigour the doctrine of belief in one God and the true idea of sin. These our Lord found ready to His hand, essential preconditions of His teaching. And in the exhibition of this great and unparalleled result of a most elaborate and peculiar discipline we may perhaps recognise, sufficiently for the present purpose, the office and work of the Old Testament.'

In another article Mr. Gladstone objects to Universalism as a contradiction of Divine utterance. He writes: 'To presume on overriding the express declarations of the Lord Himself delivered upon His own authority, is surely to break up revealed religion in its very ground-work, and to substitute for it a flimsy speculation spun like a spider's web by the private spirit, and as little capable as that web of bearing the strain by which the false is to be severed from the true.' Speaking of the theory which denies future punishment, he says: 'What is this but to emasculate all the sanctions of religion, and to give wickedness, already under a too feeble restraint, a new range of license?'

It is vain to seek to chronicle Mr. Gladstone's publications. Even at the time of his last illness he was said to have been engaged in a work on the Fathers. His writings fill six columns in the library catalogue of the British Museum.

CHAPTER XIV. ANECDOTAL AND CHARACTERISTIC.

No one has been the subject of so much small talk as Mr. Gladstone. He has been a fortune to the men who think it creditable to write gossip and twaddle for newspapers in London or the provinces. In 1881 all England was interested, or supposed to be so, in the tale of his hat. A writer says: 'The House of Commons has not had such a laugh for years as it had to-day over Mr. Gladstone and his hat. Mr. Gladstone is singular among members in never bringing a hat into the assembly. He would not wear it when his head was broken, but preferred a skull-cap. But it is the rule that after a division is called nobody shall address the Speaker standing, or with his head uncovered. To-day Mr. Gladstone wished to say something after the division-bell had rung, but no sooner did he open his mouth than the whole House yelled for him to observe the law. He sought for a hat, but could find none, the House still roaring at him. At length one of his colleagues got hold of Sir Farrer Herschell's hat and put it on him. Now, Sir Farrer is a small man among small men, and he has a small head for a small man. Mr. Gladstone, if not exactly a giant, has the head of one. Imagine him, then, with Sir Farrer's hat upon his head. A mountain crowned by a molehill could not have looked more ridiculous. The House laughed and roared at Mr. Gladstone, and Mr. Gladstone laughed at himself. Everybody voted this the sublimest spectacle of the session.' Alas! Mr. Gladstone too often lent himself in Parliament to being exhibited. To draw Gladstone was at one time a favourite sport among the young men of the Opposition. Nothing was easier. You had only to get up and misquote Mr. Gladstone, and the fiery old man was on his legs in an instant.

In the English Illustrated Magazine Mr. W. R. Lucy in 1892 gave an interesting analysis of Mr. Gladstone intellectually. He writes: 'In addition to a phenomenal physical constitution, Nature has been lavish to Mr. Gladstone in other ways. Education, association, and instinct early led him into the political arena, where he immediately made his mark. But there are half a dozen professions he might have embarked upon with equal certainty of success. Had he followed the line which one of his brothers took, he would have become a prince among the merchants of Liverpool. Had he taken to the legal profession, he would have filled the courts of law with his fame. Had he entered the Church, the highest honours would have been within his grasp. If the stage had allured him, the world would have been richer by another great actor—an opportunity, some of his critics say, not altogether lost under existing circumstances. With the personal gifts of a mobile countenance, a voice sonorous and flexible, and a fine presence, Mr. Gladstone possesses dramatic instincts frequently brought into play in House of Commons debates or in his platform speeches. In both his tendency is rather towards comedy than tragedy. It is the fashion to deny him a sense of humour, a judgment that could only be passed by a superficial observer. In private conversation his marvellous memory gives forth from its apparently illimitable stores an appropriate and frequently humorous idea of the current topic. If his fame had not been established on a loftier line, he would have been known as one of the most delightful conversationalists of the day.'

The Rev. Dr. Robertson, of Venice, having sent Mr. Gladstone a copy of his second edition of

'Fra Paolo Sarpi,' in returning thanks from Hawarden, Mr. Gladstone writes: 'I have a strong sympathy with men of his way of thinking. It pleases me particularly to be reminded of Gibbon's weighty eulogy upon his history. Ever since I read it—I think over forty years ago—I have borne to it my feeble testimony by declaring that it comes nearer to Thucydides than any historical work I have ever read. It pleases me much to learn that a Sarpi literature has appeared lately at Venice. If you were so good as to send the titles of any of the works or all works on the subject, I would order them; and I should be further glad if you would at any time thereafter come and see them in a library with hostel attached, which I am engaged in founding here.'

One of the London clubs to which Mr. Gladstone belonged was that known as Grillions, where it was the custom when a member dined there alone to record the event in verse. In 1882 Mr. Gladstone dined at the club alone, and, having written as chairman in the club-book 'one bottle of champagne,' added the following:

To which Lord Houghton, as poet-laureate of the club, added some verses, commencing:

In 1891 the Literary World wrote: 'There have been comments made lately by different writers depreciating Mr. Gladstone's literary judgments. Whatever else may be said for them, it is certain, we think, that they are not hastily formed, for in his reading, as in all else, he is strictly methodical.' This point is well made by a contributor to the Young Man, in a long and interesting article. 'Mr. Gladstone,' he says, 'cannot read hastily, nor has he ever acquired the fine art of skipping. But he is not slow to discover whether the book is worth reading, and if not, after a few pages it is cast on one side, though, as a general rule, his judgment is lenient.' In the 'Autobiography of Sir Henry Taylor' this is further illustrated. Mr. Gladstone on one occasion asked him what he thought of two or three volumes of poetry recently published. They were presentation copies sent him by obscure poets, who, if possessed of a grain or two of common-sense, could have had but little expectation that their volumes would be opened by Mr. Gladstone, even if they should pass beyond the sifting hands of his secretaries. 'He seemed, however, to be prepared to discuss their merits, had not my entire ignorance,' writes Sir Henry, 'stopped the way.'

Another characteristic is mentioned by Sir Henry on the authority of Mrs. Gladstone—the power he possessed of turning from what was arduous and anxious, and becoming at once intensely occupied with what was neither, and she regarded this as having something of a saving virtue. But she added, nevertheless, it was a frightful life.

'Gladstone's method of impartiality is,' wrote Lord Houghton, 'to be furiously earnest on both sides of a question.' Again, we have another characteristic from Lord Houghton—Gladstone saying 'he felt strongly that the statesman was becoming every day more and more the delegate of the people and less the leader.'

Another characteristic incident is recorded by Mr. Richard Redgrave: 'Mr. Lowe said that a few days before, dining with Mr. Gladstone, a lady being seated between them, Mr. Gladstone across said to Mr. Lowe: "I cannot think why they called Cobden the Inspired Bagman." "Neither can I," said Mr. Lowe; "for he was neither inspired nor a bagman. In fact, it reminds me of a story told of Madame Maintenon when someone offered to obtain an order for her to gain admission into the Maison des filles repenties. 'Nay,' said Madame, 'I am neither a fille nor am I a repentie.'" At that the lady between the two politicians burst into a laugh, but Mr. Gladstone pulled rather a long face,' as he did, I am told by a late Minister, at a dinner where Lord Westbury uttered some rather coarse jokes.

The late Mr. R. H. Hutton, of the Spectator, in an article in the Contemporary Review, smartly hit off one of Mr. Gladstone's characteristics: 'There is a story that one of his most ardent followers said of him that he did not at all object to Mr. Gladstone's always having one ace up his sleeve, but he did object to his always saying that Providence placed it there.' In 1832 a Dean of Peterborough said of Mr. Gladstone: 'His conscience is too tender ever to run straight.' In 1866 Dr. Lake, of Durham, remarked of Mr. Gladstone that 'his intellect could persuade his conscience of anything.'

'In the course of life,' Mr. Gladstone wrote to Sir Henry Taylor, 'I have found it just as difficult to get out of office as to get in, and I have done more doubtful things to get out than to get in. Furthermore, for more than nine or ten months of the year I am always willing to go, but in the two or three which precede the Budget I begin to feel an itch to have the handling of it. Last summer I should have been delighted [to resign]; now I am indifferent. In February, if I live so long, I shall, I have no doubt, be loath, but in April quite ready again. Such are my signs of the Zodiac.'

In the series of sketches of 'Bookworms of Yesterday and To-day,' place in the Bookworm is given to Mr. Gladstone, who has been a book-collector for over three-quarters of a century. 'He kindly informs me,' writes Mr. W. Roberts, 'that he has two books which he acquired in 1815, one of which was a present from Miss H. More. At the present time he estimates his library to contain from 22,000 to 25,000 books, arranged by himself into divisions and sections in a very minute manner. The library is so exceedingly miscellaneous that Mr. Gladstone himself does not venture to state which section preponderates, although he thinks that "theology may be one-fourth." There are about twenty editions of Homer, and from thirty to forty translations, whole or part. He has never sympathized to any considerable extent with the craze for modern first editions, but "I like a tall copy" is Mr. Gladstone's reply, made with all the genuine spirit of the true connoisseur, to an inquiry on the subject. And so far as regards a preference for ancient authors, in old but good editions, to modernized reprints, the verdict is emphatically in favour of the former.'

Lord Shaftesbury seems to have been struck with Mr. Gladstone's inconsistency. In his diary, in 1873, he writes: 'Last year Gladstone, speaking on Female Suffrage, said "the Bill will destroy the very foundation of social life." This year he says: "We had better defer it till we get the ballot; then it will be quite safe."' In 1864 his lordship had written: 'Mr. Gladstone will succumb to every pressure except the pressure of a constitutional and Conservative party.'

Mr. W. Lucy thus illustrates Mr. Gladstone's restlessness: 'Except at the very best, Mr. Gladstone's Parliamentary manner lacked repose. He was always brimming over with energy, which had much better have been reserved for worthier objects than those that sometimes succeeded in evoking its lavish expenditure. I once followed Mr. Gladstone through the hours of an eventful sitting. . . . The foe opposite was increasing in the persistence of his attack, and nominal friends on the benches were growing weary in their allegiance. The Premier came in from behind the chair with hurried pace; he had been detained in Downing Street up to the last moment. As usual, when contemplating making a great speech, he had a flower in his button-hole, and was dressed with unusual care. Striding swiftly past his colleagues on the Treasury Bench, he dropped into the seat kept vacant for him, and, hastily taking up a copy of the orders, ascertained what particular question in the long list had been reached. Then turning with a sudden bound of his whole body, he entered into animated conversation with a colleague, his pale face working with excitement, his eyes glistening, and his right hand vehemently beating the open palm of his left hand, as if he were literally pulverizing an adversary. Tossing himself back with equally rapid gesture, he lay passive for the space of eighty seconds. Then with another swift movement of the body he turned to the colleague on the left, dashed his hand into his side-pocket, as if he had suddenly become conscious of a live coal secreted there, pulled out a letter, opened it with a violent flick of extended forefingers, and earnestly discoursed thereon.'

In acknowledging a copy of a recently published work on 'Clergymen's Sore Throat,' Mr. Gladstone has addressed a letter to the author, Dr. E. B. Shuldham, on the subject of the management of the voice in public speaking. 'No part of the work,' writes Mr. Gladstone, 'surprised me more than your account of the various expedients resorted to by eminent singers. There, if anywhere, we might have anticipated something like a fixed tradition. But it seems we have learned nothing from experience, and I myself can testify that even in this matter fashion prevails. Within my recollection an orange, or more than one, was alone, as a rule, resorted to by members of Parliament requiring aid. Now it is never used. When I have had very lengthy statements to make I have used what is called egg-flip—a glass of sherry beaten up with an egg. I think it excellent, but I have much more faith in the egg than in the alcohol. I never think of employing it unless on the rare occasions when I have expected to go much beyond an hour. One strong reason for using something of the kind is the great exhaustion often consequent on protracted expectation and attention before speaking.'

One of the best of the many stories connected with Mr. Gladstone's many residences in the South of France tells how one Sunday he and his wife were seated in the church at Cannes near the pulpit. The Grand Old Man, turning to his wife, said, in an irritable tone: 'I can't hear.' 'Never mind, my dear,' said the lady. 'Go to sleep; it will do you much more good.'

In a chapter of his autobiography Mr. Gladstone wrote: 'In theory, and at least for others, I am a purist with respect to what touches the consistency of statesmen. Change of opinion in those to whom the public look more or less to assert its own is an evil to the country at large, though a much smaller one than their persistency in a course which they know to be wrong. It is not always to be blamed, but it is to be watched with vigilance—always to be challenged and put upon trial.'

In 1881 Mr. Gladstone told the electors of Leeds he had been a Liberal since 1846. The fact is, as Mr. Jennings has shown, that he held office under a Conservative Premier, that he was returned for Oxford as a Conservative, and that in 1858 he canvassed the county of Flint for Sir

Stephen Glynne, who was a strong supporter of Lord Derby's Government.

In 1855, when Lord Aberdeen, who was certainly no Whig, retired, Mr. Gladstone wrote a most effective letter of regret, which incidentally throws a little light on his correspondent's character. Mr. Gladstone writes: 'You make too much of services I have rendered you. I wish it were in my power to do justice in return for the benefits I have received from you. Your whole demeanour has been a living lesson to me, and I have never gone, with my vulnerable temper and impetuous moods, into your presence without feeling the strong influence of your calm and settled spirit.'

Pearson's Magazine tells some interesting things about the Grand Old Man. Though possessing strict views on Sunday observance, he does not disapprove of Sunday cycling. The bicycle, he says, is no more than a perfect means of locomotion. Hawarden Park, which is closed to ordinary tourists on Sunday, is open to cyclists. He gives the first place among living writers of fiction to Zola, but his favourite English books are the Waverley Novels. Of his once large collection of axes only thirty or forty now remain. 'In bygone days admirers were constantly sending him axes as marks of their esteem, and now other admirers quite as constantly smuggle them away as treasured mementoes of their visits.' A silver pencil, axe-shaped, presented by the Princess of Wales 'for axing questions,' is among the treasures of the G.O.M. Fifty or sixty walking-sticks, part of a once unique collection, adorn a rack outside Mr. Gladstone's study, but the number of these also 'is being diminished by visitors whose enthusiasm is in advance of their scruples.' Alluding to Mr. Gladstone's fondness for fresh air, the writer (Mr. W. A. Woodward) says: 'I have seen him, with Mrs. Gladstone at his side, a ridiculously small umbrella held between them, set forth for a pleasure drive in such torrents of rain as no ordinary mortal would have faced save on some vital·purpose.' Books on divorce and marriage—judging by the number of annotations in his neat, distinct handwriting in such volumes in his library—receive his closest attention, but he has no very great interest in the modern analytical novel. 'It is natural,' says the writer, 'that the subject of marriage, in its middle relation to politics and religion, should have exercised a large fascination over so ardent a student of theology and sociology.'

Mr. Gladstone planted a young tree at Studley Royal, and the Studley and Oldfield children were specially summoned to the place to witness the ceremonial. As they were standing in review order—there being in all about one hundred and twenty youngsters—Mr. and Mrs. Gladstone passed down the lines, and some remarks by the right hon. gentleman were addressed to Lord Ripon. The point mainly dwelt upon was the large size of the heads of Yorkshire children. Mr. Gladstone suggested that it was indicative of independence. He added that his experience was that the farther north he went, the larger he found the human head, and he told an anecdote about a man who went to a hatter's, but failed to get a hat large enough, until the tradesman, driven to desperation, called for an Aberdeen hat.

It is well known that Mr. Gladstone is an authority in the ceramic art, and he never loses an opportunity of inspecting rare and beautiful specimens. When he lately visited Manchester he spent an early hour at the exhibition among the beautiful collection placed there by Messrs.

Doulton. And there he received an unexpected pleasure. More than a dozen years ago, when speaking at a dinner of the Turners' Company, he alluded to a visit he had made to the works of Messrs. Doulton. He had been taken into the room of a young man, who happened to be absent at the time, to see the quality of his workmanship. He was delighted with what he saw, the more when he learned that the young artist had not heard a sound since his fourth year. He spoke so kindly of him and his work that it almost seemed as if Mr. Gladstone envied the isolation which seemed to favour abstraction and study in the midst of bustle and din. It was this gentleman, Mr. Frank Butler, whom Mr. Gladstone found in charge of the Doulton art treasures at Manchester. He at once remembered him, and, before leaving, he had Mr. Butler to seat himself at the potter's wheel, and fashion before him a vase as a specimen of his skill. Upon this Mr. Gladstone inscribed his name in the wet clay, and another was turned for Mrs. Gladstone.

From a little volume—'Mr. Gladstone in the Evening of his Days'—I take the following:

'Another reason why Mr. Gladstone gets through such an astounding amount of work is his extraordinary habit of using up odds and ends of time. One day not long ago he was driving into Chester after luncheon; his pudding was very hot, so he went away from table, changed his clothes, got ready for his drive, and came back and finished the meal, thus saving the ten minutes during which his pudding cooled. It may here be mentioned, in connection with the drives to Chester, that on the day a few months ago when he drove in for the purpose of making his powerful Armenian speech, Mr. Gladstone had been absorbed in Butler all the morning, and the speech was made without any special preparation.' Even at the great age of eighty-five it was evident that Mr. Gladstone worked more hours a day than many men in the prime of life would like.

Sir Francis Doyle once asked Mr. Gladstone whether, after his long years of practice, he ever felt nervous on rising to speak. 'Not on political questions,' was his answer; 'but if I am called upon to deliver what the Greeks used to call an "epideictic oration," as at the Literary Fund dinner, or the like, I am often somewhat troubled at first.'

'I have just heard,' wrote on one occasion a correspondent of the Manchester Guardian, 'a highly characteristic anecdote of Mr. Gladstone's versatility. I suppress the name and place. After an interesting interview with a prominent author, whose acquaintance he had newly made, in reply to a courteous hope that his health and strength might long be spared, Mr. Gladstone said: "Yes, I confess I wish to live for two great objects. You can guess one of them: it is to settle the Irish question. The other is, to convince my countrymen of the substantial identity between the theology of Homer and that of the Old Testament."'

Under this heading we give a few items from Bishop Wilberforce's notes. In 1868 he writes: 'Gladstone noble as ever.' Again: 'Gladstone, as ever, just, earnest, and honest, as unlike the tricky Disraeli as ever.' Again the Bishop writes, after staying with him at Hatfield: 'I have very much enjoyed meeting Gladstone. He is so delightfully true—just as full of interest in every good thing of every kind, and exactly the reverse of the mystery man. When people talk of Gladstone going mad, they do not take into account the wonderful elasticity of his mind and the variety of his interests. Now, this morning after breakfast he and I and Salisbury went a walk round the beautiful park, and he was just as much interested in the size of the oaks, their probable age, etc., as if no care of State ever pressed upon him. This is his safeguard, joined to rectitude of purpose and clearness of view.'

No reference to Mr. Gladstone would be complete without a word about his collars. In a paper on the subject in the New Century, Mr. Harry Furniss writes: 'I believe I am generally supposed to have invented Mr. Gladstone's collars; but, as a matter of fact, I merely sketched them. Many men wear collars quite as large, and even larger, than his, but they are not so prominent in appearance, for the simple reason that when Mr. Gladstone sits down it is his custom to sit well forward; his body collapsed, so to speak, and his head sunk into his seat. The inevitable result was that his collar rose, and owing to this circumstance I have frequently seen it looking quite as conspicuous as it is depicted in my caricatures. When Mr. Gladstone upon one occasion met the artists of Punch at dinner, I was chagrined to find when he walked into the dining-room that he had discarded his usual large collar for one of the masher type. I felt that my reputation for accuracy was blighted, and sought consolation from the editor of a Gladstonian organ who happened to be present. "Yes," he said; "he is evidently dressed up to meet the Punch artists. He is the pink of fashion and neatness now; but last night when I met him at dinner his shirt was frayed at the edges, and his collar was pinned down behind, but the pin gave way during the evening, and the collar nearly came over his head."'

Mr. Justin McCarthy has much to say of Mr. Gladstone's eyes: 'I am myself strongly of opinion that Mr. Gladstone strongly improved in appearance as his life went on deepening into years. I cannot, of course, remember him as he was in 1833. I think I saw him for the first time some twenty years later. But although he was a decidedly handsome man at that time, I did not think his appearance was nearly so striking or so commanding as it became in the closing years of his career. I do not believe that I ever saw a more magnificent human face than that of Mr. Gladstone after he had grown old. Of course, the eyes were always superb. Many a stranger looking at Mr. Gladstone for the first time saw the eyes, and only the eyes, and could think for a moment of nothing else. Age never dimmed the fire of these eyes.'

A few characteristics are given by Mr. McCarthy: 'I have mixed,' he writes, 'with most of Mr. Gladstone's contemporaries, his political opponents as well as his political followers, and I have never heard a hint of any serious defect in his nature, or of any unworthy motive influencing his private or public career. Defects of temperament, and of manner, and of tact have no doubt been ascribed to him over and over again. He was not, people tell me, always successful in playing up to or conciliating the weaknesses of inferior men. He was not good, I am told, at remembering faces or names. . . . Such defects, however, in Mr. Gladstone's nature or temperament count indeed for little or nothing in the survey of his career.' Another characteristic of Mr. Gladstone, remarks Mr. McCarthy, is his North-country accent.

Sir Andrew Clark, who was Mr. Gladstone's physician for years, said he never had a more docile patient than Mr. Gladstone. The moment he is really laid up he goes to bed, and there remains till he recovers. He is a firm believer in the doctrine of lying in bed when you are ill. You keep yourself in an equable temperature, avoid the worries and drudgery of everyday life, and being in bed is a good pretext for avoiding the visits of the multitude of people whose room is better than their company.

Mr. Gladstone's admirers are very angry when it is intimated that his character is not perfection. It may be there are spots in the sun, but the idol of the party must be spotless.

The following anecdote illustrates Mr. Gladstone's love of music. On the eve of one of his great budgets, Mr. Gladstone found time to go to the theatre to see Sarah Bernhardt act in 'Phèdre.' The great statesman was so delighted with the acting, that he wrote to mademoiselle a letter expressing his great gratification. The divine Sarah always had a great influence on the impressionable Premier. When she held a reception, the first to come and the last to go was Mr. Gladstone, and none who witnessed it were likely to forget the spectacle of the great statesman bending low almost till he kissed the hand of the actress when she advanced to welcome him.

According to all accounts, Mr. Gladstone is on the most friendly terms with his tenantry. To some of them he has been specially kind. On the occasion of the marriage of his son and heir he feasted 550 of his cottage tenants on the first day, and upwards of 400 on the second. On one occasion, while Mr. Gladstone was pointing out to a large party of excursionists the beauties of the trees, he added: 'We are very proud of our trees.' 'Why, then, do you cut them down as you do?' said a man in the crowd. Said the Grand Old Man in reply: 'We cut down that we may improve. We remove rottenness that we may restore health by letting in air and light. As a good Liberal, you ought to understand that.'

Again I give an anecdote of his kindness as landlord. When Mr. Gladstone was engaged in one of his Midlothian campaigns, his principal tenant, an energetic and capable practical farmer, was suffering from severe illness. Every day during the campaign came a letter from Mr. and Mrs. Gladstone inquiring after his health. On their return from Scotland, having travelled all night, they drove from Chester straight to the tenant's house, and were both in his bedroom at half-past eight in the morning.

Another Hawarden anecdote may be recorded here. In Mr. Gladstone's household was an old woman-servant, who had a son inclined to go wrong. The mother remonstrated, but all to no purpose. At last she thought if the Premier would take the prodigal in hand, at last he might be reclaimed. She appealed to Mr. Gladstone, and he responded at once to her appeal. He had the lad sent to his study, spoke to him words of tender advice and remonstrance, and eventually knelt down with him and prayed to a higher Power to help in the work of reformation.

In May, 1885, Mr. Lucy writes: 'In making a statement to-night on the course of public business, the Premier spoke, as has been a matter of custom of late, amid continuous noisy interruptions from a section of the Conservative party. To-night this method of Parliamentary procedure, novel, as directed against the leader of the House, reached a climax which had the desired effect of temporarily silencing the Premier. After a painful pause, he observed that this new kind of Parliamentary warfare was of little matter to him, whose personal interposition in political strife was a question of weeks rather than of months, certainly of months more than of years. But he had a deep conviction that within the last three years a blow had been struck at the liberty and dignity of the House of Commons by these intrusions upon debate.'

No notice can be held to be complete which does not give one an idea of the splendid physical constitution which has enabled Mr. Gladstone to lead the life he has led and to do the work he has done. On one occasion he told his Welsh admirers that it was due to the air of that part of the Principality near which he resided. But his vitality is undoubtedly an illustration of the principle of heredity. The medical journals had always much to say of Mr. Gladstone's health. We quote one. At the end of the session in which Mr. Gladstone carried his Irish Land Bill, the Lancet wrote: 'Apart from all party and political considerations, it is but proper to express our satisfaction at seeing Mr. Gladstone, at the end of a session almost unprecedented for length and for those influences which harass and exhaust, in a state of admirable health and spirits. It was a physiological and psychological marvel last week to see him rise and show reasons for disagreeing with the Lords' Amendments, not in any hasty or excited mood, but with perfect serenity of intellect and temper, with absolute mastery of details, and appealing to all that was best in his opponents. This is a feat which exceeds, in our judgment, the felling of many trees, and almost crowns Mr. Gladstone's many claims to distinction. The last straw breaks the camel's back, and it would have been excusable if the obstructions of August had elicited peevishness and intelligible if they had produced exhaustion. But both strength and temper are intact, and Mr. Gladstone goes to his holiday with a stock of energy which many younger men would be glad to return with, and which is no mean guarantee for future service to his Queen and country.'

Archbishop Magee used to tell a good story of Father Healy and Mr. Gladstone. The latter asked him upon what principle the Roman Church offered soul indulgences, saying when he was in Rome he was offered an indulgence for fifty francs. Father Healy replied: 'Well, Mr. Gladstone, I do not want to go into theology with you; but all I can say is, that if my Church offered you an indulgence for fifty francs, she let you off very cheap!'

A correspondent, a well-known London minister, who got crushed in the crowd at the opening of St. Martin's Free Library, in 1891, by Mr. Gladstone, tells an anecdote of the ex-Premier's kindness of heart, on the authority of a former vicar. When Chancellor of the Exchequer, Mr. Gladstone regularly attended this church. A crossing-sweeper in the parish, who had been some time ill, when asked by the vicar if anybody had been to see him, said, 'Yes, sir; Mr. Gladstone.' 'Which Mr. Gladstone?' he was asked. 'Why,' was the answer, 'Mr. Gladstone himself. He often speaks to me, and gives me something at my crossing. Not seeing me, he asked my mate, who was keeping it for me, why I was not there. He told him I was ill, and then he asked where I lived. So he came to see me, and talked and read to me.'

There was a characteristic big gathering, deserving to be recorded here, at the National Liberal Club, in celebration of Mr. and Mrs. Gladstone's golden wedding. In all there were nearly 2,000 guests, and these included most of the Liberal leaders, and at least one distinguished Liberal Unionist (Sir John Lubbock), who, when perceived among the throng, received the welcome of a cordial cheer. The chief feature of the proceedings was the presentation of the handsome commemorative album—a remarkable work of art—to the ex-Premier in the reading-room. The scene here was a particularly brilliant one; and when Mr. and Mrs. Gladstone appeared among the throng, accompanied by several members of the family, there was an outburst of enthusiasm which was continued to an unwonted length. Mr. Gladstone's reply to the address was not long; it was a feelingly-uttered expression of gratification. Only a few sentences were occupied with political allusions. They declared that Liberal principles were not of destruction, but of improvement.

These are a few of the sentences of thanks: 'I am ashamed,' said Mr. Gladstone, 'of the kindness that has been shown me. ("No.") When I speak of my wife, when I acknowledge that there is greater justice in the tributes that you have so kindly paid to her, I there enjoy a relative and a comparative freedom, and no words that I could use would ever suffice to express the debt that I owe her in relation to all the offices that she has discharged on my behalf, and on the behalf of those who are near and dearest to us, during the long and happy period of our conjugal union. (Cheers.) I hope it will not sound like exaggeration—it is really a phrase dictated by my desire to express what I feel—if I say that I feel myself to be, as it were, drowned in an ocean of kindness.'

The other day Canon Scott Holland, in a touching sermon, described Mr. Gladstone as 'spending his life in benedictions to those whom he leaves behind in this world, and in thanksgiving to God, to whom he rehearses over and over again, day after day, Newman's hymn of austere and splendid admiration.' Here is the hymn:

At other times Mr. Gladstone has been known to say that his favourite hymns were 'Rock of Ages' and the version of 'Dies Iræ' which Scott introduced into 'The Lay of the Last Minstrel':

Mr. Gladstone, according to a writer in the Daily News, once remarked that he had made a careful study of all Toplady's hymns, but had only found four other good lines in the whole of them. To those who have ever heard Mr. Gladstone recite these four lines, as he was often used to do, the recollection will come just now with pathetic poignancy:

For Charles Wesley's hymns Mr. Gladstone did not greatly care. He considered them much over-rated. 'And he wrote more than Homer,' exclaimed Mr. Gladstone once; '7,000 hymns of thirty lines each, say; do the sum, gentlemen, and be appalled.'

CHAPTER XV. MR. GLADSTONE'S LETTERS.

To this Mr. Bright replied two days afterwards as follows:

At the St. Asaph Diocesan Conference the following letter, addressed by the Premier to Dr. Hughes, Bishop of St. Asaph, was read by Canon Wynne Edwards:

During the subsequent proceedings the letter was frequently referred to as a magnificent letter, and as one worthy of the Premier's transcendent abilities.

Mr. Gladstone wrote to Lord E. Fitzmaurice, complimenting him upon a speech which he delivered at Old Cumnock, in Ayrshire. 'It was pre-eminently,' said the ex-Premier, 'the speech that was wanted, made by one who was "in all respects peculiarly the man to make it." In my view,' proceeded Mr. Gladstone, 'Ireland is the heading of a bright chapter in the history, not only of the Liberals, but especially of the Whigs. It was a noble thing on the part of Burke and Fitzwilliam and the other seceders from Fox that not all their horror of France could make them untrue to Ireland. The Whig party after the schism remained for Irish purposes unbroken, and were right in each one of the various stages through which the question had to pass—right in the endeavour, frustrated by Pitt and the ascendency men, to work the Grattan Parliament; right in the opposition to the Union when it was shamelessly forced on Ireland; right in saying, by the mouth of Fox, that so huge a measure must have an unprejudiced and a full trial when it had once been effected, and when no man could undertake to say positively that Ireland might not come, as Scotland had come, to make it her own by adoption; right, probably, when Grattan gave his provisional sanction to coercion as the necessary sequel to the Union; right certainly when Lord Grey and Lord Althorp proposed further coercion in 1834, when they had done, and were doing, for Ireland in so many ways all which at the time they could, and when no Minister was in a condition to say constitutionally that the sense of the Irish people demanded self-government; and, finally, right was a cruelly crippled remnant of their leading class, enthusiastically supported from first to last by a large portion of the nation, in listening to the constitutional demand of Ireland by their representatives in 1885, and in recognising after three generations had passed away that union with coercion—in other words, government by force—had been tried all but too fully, and had entirely failed. We want,' continued Mr. Gladstone, 'a little Whig treatment of Ireland.' Dealing with another aspect of the argument, which he characterized as 'not less unacceptable and important,' he expressed the fear that the action of the chief part of the Whig peers and aristocracy in severing themselves from the bulk of the Liberal party might be to narrow the Liberal party, which had hitherto been so broad. This he attributed 'entirely to the so-called Liberal Unionists.' 'Liberal Unionism has,' he said, 'tended to break up the old and invaluable habit of Liberal England, which looked to a Liberal aristocracy and a Liberal leisured class as the natural, and therefore the best, leaders of the Liberal movement. Thus it was that classes and masses were united.' This controversy, and the recollection, will do away with the certain triumph of Home Rule. But will the ranks which have been divided easily close up? 'I, for one,' repeated Mr. Gladstone, 'think that the narrowing of the party by the severance or reduction of one wing is also the crippling of the party.'

Mr. Gladstone had, as he himself put it, 'felt it his duty to put Liberal candidates in possession of some means of meeting statements' as to his past connection with the Tory party. The particular remark which elicited this letter was made by Mr. Chatterton, the Tory candidate for the Crewe division. It was that 'in his fiftieth year Mr. Gladstone was in full sympathy with the Tory party.' Mr. Gladstone, in his letter, put forward ten propositions: 'It is true that down to the year 1839, when I was twenty-nine years old, I might fairly be called a Tory of the Tories in questions relating to the Church. (2) It is untrue that even at that time I could justly be so described in other questions. (3) I am not aware that after 1839, or, at all events, after 1841, I could justly be described, even in Church questions, as a Tory of the Tories, or perhaps as a Tory at all. (4) In 1843 I was denounced in the House of Lords as being disloyal to the principles of Protection. (5) In 1849–50 I assisted to the best of my power the Government of Naples. (6) In 1851, in company with the Peelites, the Irish Roman Catholics, and the group led by Mr. Cobden, I actively resisted both Whigs and Tories, but the last especially, in defence of religious liberty, on the Ecclesiastical Titles Bill. (7) Unquestionably I differed strongly from the first Government of Lord Palmerston in 1855–8, on the question of peace, of foreign policy, of finance, and of divorce. The last was not a party question. On the other three I believe that my opinions were, as they are now, practically the opinions of the Liberal party. (8) Lord Derby sent me to the Ionian Islands in 1858, in precisely the same sense as that in which the Government of 1868–74 sent Lord Iddesleigh to America. (9) In company with Lord Russell and Mr. Milner Gibson, I gave the vote in 1858 on the Conspiracy Bill which brought in the Tories. Like Lord Russell, after doing this, I knew it to be my duty to give the Tories fair-play and such support as was equitable until positive cause of difference should arise. (10) Before their Italian policy was made public, I declined to join in the vote of want of confidence which removed them from office. But a few weeks later, when the volume containing it was published, I intimated in Parliament that had I known that policy at the time I should have pursued a different course.' 'So much,' adds Mr. Gladstone, 'for my Toryism down to 1859.'

In 1876 Mr. Gladstone wrote to Hayward: 'The Times appears to be thoroughly emasculated. It does not pay to read a paper which next week is sure to refute what it has demonstrated this week. It ought to be prohibited to change sides more than a certain number of times in a year. As to the upper ten thousand, it has not been by a majority of that body that any of the great and good measures of our century have been carried, though a minority have done good service; and so I fear it will continue.' Mr. Gladstone seems in 1878 to have had a poor opinion of the Daily News. 'I think,' he wrote to Blachford, 'they have often made improper admissions, and do not drive the nail home as it really ought to be done by a strong Opposition paper, such as the Morning Chronicle of Derry.'

In his address to the electors of Midlothian in 1886, Mr. Gladstone said: 'Lord Hartington has lately and justly stated in general terms that he is not disposed to deny our having fallen into errors of judgment. I will go one step further, and admit that we committed such errors, and serious errors, too, with cost of treasure and of precious lives, in the Soudan. For none of these errors were we rebuked by the voice of the Opposition; we were only rebuked, and that incessantly, because we did not commit them with precipitation, and because we did not commit other errors greater still. Our mistakes in the Soudan I cannot now state in detail; the task belongs to history. Our responsibility for them cannot be questioned; yet its character ought not to be misapprehended. In such a task miscarriages were inevitable. They are the proper and certain consequence of undertakings that war against nature, and that lie beyond the scope of human means, and of rational and prudent human action; and the first authors of these undertakings are the real makers of the mischief.'

In connection with this subject, let us add the following from Gordon's Diary at Khartoum: 'Poor Gladstone's Government! how they must love me! I will accept nothing whatever from Gladstone's hands. I will not let them even pay my expenses; I will get the King to pay them. I will never set foot in England again.'

Perhaps one of the most remarkable letters a great statesman ever wrote was that to an American in 1862, in which Mr. Gladstone thus shows how impossible it was for the North to put down the South. He writes: 'You know, in the opinion of Europe, that impossibility has been proved. Depend upon it, to place the matter on a simple issue, you cannot conquer and keep down a country where the women behave like the women of New Orleans, and when a writer says they would be ready to form regiments, were such regiments required. And how idle it is to talk as some of your people do, and some of ours, of the slackness with which the war has been carried on, and of its accounting for the want of success. You have no cause to be ashamed of your military character and efforts. . . . I am, in short, a follower of General Scott; with him I say, Wayward sisters, go in peace. Immortal fame be to him for his wise and courageous advice, amounting to a prophecy. Finally, you have done what man could do; you have failed because you have resolved to do what man could not do. Laws stronger than human will are on the side of earnest self-defence; and to aim at the impossible, which in other things may be folly only when the path of search is dark with misery and red with blood, is not folly only, but guilt to boot.'

In 1880 some correspondence was published between Captain Boycott and Mr. Gladstone. The former wrote to the Prime Minister, giving a narrative of the events which obliged him to leave Ireland, and asked for compensation from the Government. 'I have been prevented from pursuing my business peaceably; where my property has not been stolen, it has been maliciously wasted, and my life has been in hourly peril for many months. I have been driven from my home, and, having done no evil, find myself a ruined man, because the law as administered has not protected me.' In reply, Mr. Gladstone's secretary wrote: 'Mr. Gladstone has received your letter of the 8th inst., and, in reply, desires me to say that he is not sure in what way he is to understand your request for assistance from her Majesty's Government. It has been very largely afforded you in the use of the public force; beyond this it is the duty of the Government to use its best exertions in the enforcement of the existing law, which they are endeavouring to effect through the courts, and by asking when necessary the assistance of the Legislature to amend or enlarge the law—a matter of much importance, on which you can, of course, only receive information together with the public generally.' A little later we were informed Mr. Gladstone declined to accede to Captain Boycott's claim for pecuniary compensation on account of having to leave his farm, holding that the large display of public force required for Captain Boycott's protection having been furnished, the State could not be expected to entertain any further claims.

Mr. Gladstone addressed the following letter to the editor of the Baptist:

Mr. Gladstone's secretary, writing to a correspondent in the Daily News in 1885, who had asked what the clergy were drawing from national funds, replied: 'Sir,—Mr. Gladstone, in reply to your letter, desires me to inform you that the clergy are not State paid.'

Again, to a correspondent Mr. Gladstone wrote: 'You are mistaken in supposing that the outrages in Manchester and Clerkenwell determined or affected my action with regard to Ireland. They drew the attention of the public, on which there are so many demands, to Irish questions, and thereby enabled me in point of time to act in a manner for which I had previously declared my desire. You state that the Irish voters are preparing themselves to punish the Liberal party. In that respect I do not see that those of whom you speak can improve upon what they have already done; for in and since 1874, just after that party had dealt with the questions of Church and Land, they inflicted upon it the heaviest Parliamentary blow it has received in my time. I hope, however, from every present indication, that, notwithstanding the mischief done to it and to the wider interests of humanity by the Irish secession, it will, when an opportunity is allowed, prove to have strength sufficient for the exigencies of the time.'

CHAPTER XVI. MR. GLADSTONE AND HIS CONTEMPORARIES.

In 1853 Lord Blachford wrote, just after Mr. Gladstone had unfolded his famous Budget which took off newspapers the additional stamp required for supplements, and imposed a single stamp of a penny for every newspaper of whatever sort: 'If Gladstone has anything Conservative in him, he will find it difficult to remain in a Ministry which must eventually be thrown upon Radical support. But he is really so powerful a man that, whatever shakes and delays and loss of time there may be, he must come up near the surface. I expect he will show the best—i.e., most politically powerful—side of himself as Chancellor of the Exchequer. Pursuing details is so much his power if he is only not run away with by it. I think, if it is not a paradox, he has not poetry enough for the formation of a first-rate judgment. He has an immense mass of knowledge most methodically arranged, but the separate items must be looked for in their respective boxes, and do not combine. The consequence is not merely want of play, but that crotchety, one-sided, narrowish mode of viewing a matter uncorrected by the necessary comparisons and considerations which people call ingenious and subtle and Gladstonian. He looks at the details, not at the aspects of a subject, and masters it, I should imagine, by pursuing it hither and thither from one starting-point, and not by walking round it; and financial subjects will, I suppose, bear this mode of treatment better than any other.'

In a valuable work by a distinguished German, Dr. Geiffeken, of which an English translation appeared in 1889, the author thus described Mr. Gladstone: 'His eloquence shows as its prominent quality the acuteness of intelligent methodical thought, and a readiness which, united with the most complete mastery of the matter, seems to require no preparation. He is beyond all cavil the first speaker of his time on subjects connected with public business, and is unsurpassed in power of luminous presentation of complicated economic questions. Relying on a memory that never fails, he knows how to impart life to the dryest array of figures, to group them in attractive forms, and to expound them so that his hearers may have them completely within their grasp. Nor is he less able in mastering the most involved question of law. His imagination is short-winded, dry, and apt to lose itself in speculation. His pathos is without warmth, his diction lacks charm, in spite of his copious command of language, his clear periods, and the inexhaustible staying power of his voice. The most unfavourable side of him as a speaker is seen when he begins to argue. Mr. Escobar never understood so well as he how to use language against the use of language, to involve his thoughts in clouds, to explain away inconvenient facts, to leave himself a back-door open to escape, and to father upon his opponents assertions which they would in nowise acknowledge. He involves the truth so hopelessly that it is impossible to disentangle it.'

Sir Rowland Hill, in his 'Autobiography,' writes: 'There are few public men with whom I have not come on such excellent terms, and from whom I have received so much kindness, as from Mr. Gladstone.'

Archbishop Trench, writing to Bishop Wilberforce in 1864, says: 'I deeply regret Mr. Gladstone's Reform speech, which certainly may alter his future—may alter the whole future of

England. No man but one endowed with his genius and virtues could effectually do mischief to the institutions of England, but he may do it.' Again he wrote: 'Nothing can hinder Mr. Gladstone from being the most remarkable man in England.'

In the autumn of 1859 Sir Archibald Alison, the historian, met Mr. Gladstone at the hospitable mansion of Mr. Stirling, of Keir, near Stirling. 'I had been acquainted with him,' he writes, 'when he was a young man, and he had dined once or twice at our house in St. Colome Street, but I had not seen him for above twenty years, and in the interval he had become a leading Parliamentary orator and a great man. I was particularly observant, therefore, of his manner and conversation, and I was by no means disappointed in either. In manner he had the unaffected simplicity of earlier days, without either the assumption of superiority which might have been natural from his Parliamentary eminence, or the official pedantry so common in persons who have held high office in the State. In conversation he was rapid, easy and fluent, and possessed in a high degree that great quality so characteristic of a powerful mind, so inestimable in discoursing, of quickly apprehending what was said on the other side, and in reply setting himself at once to meet it fairly and openly. He was at once energetic and discursive, enthusiastic, but at times visionary. It was impossible to listen to him without pleasure, but equally so to reflect on what he said without grave hesitation. He left on my mind the impression of his being the best discourser on imaginative topics, and the most dangerous person to be entrusted with practical ones, I had ever met with. He gave me more the impression of great scholastic acumen than of weighty, statesman-like wisdom. Eminent in the University, and transferred without any practical training in the school of life at once from its shades to the House of Commons, he was like the ecclesiastics who in Catholic countries were often transferred direct from the cloister to the Cabinet, and began to operate on mankind as they would do on a dead body to elucidate certain points of physics, and who have so often proved at once the ablest and most dangerous of governors.'

An able writer, Mr. Bagehot, contends Mr. Gladstone is spoilt by applause, as follows: 'But because his achievements have fallen so much below the standard of his expectations, because destiny has fought against him and proved too much for him, is Mr. Gladstone on that account dejected? On the contrary, although he may experience some passing emotions of chagrin and a pious resentment against circumstances, he cherishes the comfortable conviction that both what he has done and what he has abstained from doing are right. Facts may be against him, but, then, so much the worse for the facts. His view of foreign politics is that every male child born into the world, whether Indian or African, Mussulman, Egyptian fellah or Zulu Kaffir, Aztec or Esquimaux, is capable of being educated into a free and independent elector for an English borough. Parliamentary institutions and representative Government are to him, not only the supreme end at which to aim, but the régime to which all nationalities are instinctively capable of adapting themselves. He makes no allowance for difference of race or climate, historical antecedents, national peculiarities. Herein he displays a lack of imagination, which is more strange, seeing that he possesses a large allowance of the imaginative faculty in other respects, and that he is really poet first and statistician afterwards.

'Particular causes have combined to confirm this defect. Mr. Gladstone has spent his life in the House of Commons, and cannot imagine a political system or a scheme of popular rule without as accurate a copy as conditions permit of the English representative Chamber. Again, he understands the English people so well, he has so completely identified himself with the ideas and aspirations of the upper class of bourgeoisie, that he considers it scarcely worth while to attempt to understand any other race. If he attempts such an intellectual process he can only measure the unfamiliar by reference to the familiar object.

'Mr. Gladstone has drunk too deeply of the atmosphere of idolatry and incense by which he has been surrounded. His immense experience of public life, his great capacities as a financier, his moral earnestness, his religious fervour, his scholarship, culture, and conversational powers, have procured for him enthusiastic worshippers in every section of the community—among the lower classes; among the men of commerce and business; among the Whig aristocracy, with whom he has been educated, and who have long since seen in him the bulwark against revolution; among the clergy of the Anglican Church and the Nonconformist ministers; finally, among certain small and exclusive divisions of London society itself. No man can receive the homage that has fallen to the lot of Mr. Gladstone during so many years without experiencing a kind of moral intoxication and forming an excessive idea of his own infallibility. Nor is it good for him that domestic interposition should ward off the hostile expressions of opinions in the newspapers not attached to his cause, but which may, nevertheless, represent the views of a certain section of the English people.'

Mr. G. W. E. Russell, in his charming little book on Gladstone, refers to Mr. Gladstone's speech on the Don Pacifico debate, as illustrating his tendency 'to belittle England, to extol and magnify the virtues and graces of other nations, and to ignore the homely prejudice of patriotism. He has frankly told us that he does not know the meaning of prestige, and an English Minister who makes that confession has yet to learn one of the governing sentiments of

Whether this peculiarity of Mr. Gladstone's mind can be referred to the fact that he has not a drop of English blood in his body is perhaps a fanciful inquiry; but its consequences are plain enough in the vulgar belief that he is indifferent to the interests and honour of the country which he has three times ruled, and that his love for England is swamped and lost in the enthusiasm of humanity.'

In an article on the Peelites in Macmillan's, Professor Goldwin Smith writes: 'Gladstone does not yet belong to history, and the only part of his career which fell specially under my notice was Oxford University Reform. He opposed inquiry when a Commission was announced by Lord John Russell, and afterwards, as a member of the Coalition Government, he framed what was for that day a drastic and comprehensive measure of reform. . . . It was impossible to be brought into contact with Mr. Gladstone, even in so slight a way, without being made sensible of his immense powers of work, of mastering and marshalling details, of framing a comprehensive measure, and of carrying it against opposition in the House of Commons. I also saw and appreciated his combative energy. The Bill had been miserably mauled in the Commons by Disraeli, with the aid of some misguided Radicals. When it got to the Lords I was placed under the steps of the throne, to be at hand if information on details was needed by those in charge of the Bill. The House seemed very full, but the Duke of Newcastle came to me and said that he did not believe Lord Derby intended to venture on a real opposition to the Bill, as there had not been a strong whip on the Conservative side. "In that case," I said, "what hinders you from reversing here the amendments which have been carried against you in the Commons?" A conference was held in the library to consider this suggestion, but Lord Russell, the leader of the Commons, peremptorily vetoed it on the ground of prudence. Mr. Gladstone was confined to his room by illness, but, in compliance with my earnest prayer, the question was referred to him. Next day the signal for battle was hung out, and I had the great satisfaction of looking on while a series of amendments in committee—the Commons amendments—were reversed, and the Bill was restored to a workable state.'

In 1868 Bishop Colenso writes: 'I had a very pleasant letter by the last mail from Mr. Gladstone, to whom I wrote ten months ago with reference to his language about Bishop Gray and myself at an S.P.G. meeting at Penmaenmawr. He had my letter before him for four months, as he says, but he begs me to believe that this long interval of silence has not been due to any indifference or disrespect; and, in short, he writes a very kind and courteous letter, administering a little rebuke to me at the end, "not so much with respect to particular opinions, as to what appears to be your method (technically so called) in the treatment of theological questions."' Again, in 1881: 'I need not say that I am utterly disappointed with Mr. Gladstone and Lord Kimberley, and particularly with the tone of the Daily News, speaking, I suppose, as the Government organ. I cannot help thinking that the present Government has lost a great deal of its power by the feebleness they have shown in their action with regard to South African affairs, where, as far as I can see, they have not righted a single wrong committed by Sir B. Frere, and only withdrawn him under great pressure, and when he had already set on foot further mischief.' In a little while the Bishop writes more approvingly: 'It gives us hope that other wrongs may be redressed when Mr. Gladstone is ready, even in the midst of defeats at Laing's Neck, Ingogo, and Majuba, to hold back the hand of Great Britain from cruelly chastising these brave patriots, so unequally matched with our power, which of course could overwhelm and crush them.'

Count Bismarck is reported to have said: 'If I had done half as much harm to my country as Mr. Gladstone has done to his country the last four years, I would not dare to look my countrymen in the face.'

Mr. Kinglake thus describes Mr. Gladstone: 'If he was famous for the splendour of his eloquence, for his unaffected piety, and blameless life, he was celebrated far and wide for a more than common liveliness of conscience. He had once imagined it to be his duty to quit a Government and to burst through strong ties of friendship and gratitude by reason of a thin shade of difference on the subject of white or brown sugar. It was believed that if he were to commit even a little sin or to imagine an evil thought he would instantly arraign himself before the dread tribunal which awaited him within his own bosom, and that his intellect being subtle and microscopic, and delighting in casuistry and exaggeration, he would be likely to give his soul a very harsh trial, and treat himself as a great criminal for faults too minute to be visible to the naked eyes of laymen. His friends lived in dread of his virtues, as tending to make him whimsical and unstable, and the practical politicians, perceiving that he was not to be depended upon for party purposes, and was bent on none but lofty objects, used to look upon him as dangerous, used to call him behind his back a good man—a good man in the worst sense of the term.'

In 1865 Carlyle wrote: 'I had been at Edinburgh, and had heard Gladstone make his great oration on Homer there on retiring from office as Rector. It was a grand display. I never recognised before what oratory could do, the audience being kept for three hours in a state of electric tension, bursting every moment into applause. Nothing was said which seemed of moment when read deliberately afterwards; but the voice was like enchantment, and the street when we left the building was ringing with a prolongation of cheers.' Again he meets Gladstone at Mentone in 1867, and thus describes him: 'Talk copious, ingenious, but of no worth or sincerity; pictures, literature, finance, prosperities, greatness of outlook for Italy, etc.—a man ponderous, copious, of evident faculty, but all gone irrecoverably into House of Commons shape; man once of some wisdom or possibility of it, but now possessed by the Prince or many Princes of the Power of the Air. Tragic to me, and far from enviable, from whom one felt one's self divided by abysmal chasms and immeasurabilities.' On the passing of the measure of Irish Church Disestablishment, Carlyle writes: 'In my life I have seen few more anarchic, factious, unpatriotic achievements than this of Gladstone and his Parliament in respect to such an Ireland as now is. Poor Gladstone!' Again he writes: 'Ten days ago read Gladstone's article in the Edinburgh Review with amazement. Empty as a blown goose egg. Seldom have I read such a ridiculous, solemn, addlepated Joseph Surface of a thing. Nothingness, or near it, conscious to itself of being greatness almost unexampled. . . . According to the People's William, England with himself atop is evidently even now at the top of the world. Against bottomless anarchy in all fibres of her spiritual and practical she has now a complete ballot-box—can vote and count noses as free as air. Nothing else wanted, clearly thinks the People's William. He would ask you with unfeigned astonishment what else. The sovereign thing in nature is parmaceti (read ballot) for an inward bruise. That is evidently his belief, what he finds believable about England in 1870. Parmaceti, parmaceti—enough of him and it.' This was written in 1870.

In 1873 the old Chelsea Sage writes more bitterly still: 'The whole world is in a mighty fuss here about Gladstone and his Bill (Irish Education)—the attack on the third branch of the upas tree, and the question of what is to become of him in consequence of it. To myself, from the beginning, it seemed the consummation of contemptibilities and petty trickeries on his part; one of the most transparent bits of thimble-rigging to secure the support of his sixty Irish votes, the Pope's brass band, and to smuggle the education violin into the hands of Cullen and the sacred sons of Belial and the scarlet woman, I had ever seen from him before.' And again: 'Gladstone seems to me one of the contemptiblest men I ever looked on—a poor Ritualist, almost spectral kind of a phantasm of a man; nothing in him but forms and ceremonies and artistic mappings; incapable of seeing veritably any fact whatever, but seeing, crediting, and laying to heart the mere clothes of the fact, and fancying that all the rest does not exist. Let him fight his own battle in the name of Beelzebub, the god of Ekron, who seems to be his god. Poor phantasm!' When the catastrophe of 1874 came, and the People's William was flung from his pedestal, the general opinion was that his star had set for ever, till he saw who it was that the people had chosen to replace him. His mind misgave him then that the greater faults of his successor would lift Mr. Gladstone back again to a yet more giddy eminence and greater opportunities for evil.

'Finally,' remarks Mr. Froude, 'he did not look on Mr. Gladstone merely as an orator who, knowing nothing as it ought to be known, had flung his force into words and specious sentiments, but as the representative of the multitudinous cants of the age, religious, moral, political, literary; differing on this point from other leading men, that he believed in all, and was prepared to act on it. He, in fact, believed Mr. Gladstone to be one of those fatal figures created by England's evil genius to work irreparable mischief, which no one but he could have executed.'

In her 'Memories of Old Friends' Miss Caroline Fox tells us she asked Carlyle, 'Is not Gladstone a man of principle?' 'I did hope well of him once,' replied Carlyle, 'in 1867, and so did John Stirling, though I heard he was a Puseyite and so forth . . . and so I hoped something might come of him; but now he has been declaring that England is in such a wonderfully prosperous state—meaning that it has plenty of money in its breeches pockets and plenty of beef in its great ugly belly. But that is not the prosperity we want, and so I say to him: "You are not the lifegiver to England. I go my way; you go yours."' Mr. Froude, in his 'Oceana,' testifies to Mr. Gladstone's unpopularity in the Colonies. At Melbourne, at the time of the Gordon catastrophe, he writes: 'They did not love him before, and had been at a loss to understand the influence which he had so long exercised. His mighty popularity must, they thought, now be at an end. It could not survive a wound so deadly in his country's reputation. They were deceived, it seems,' adds Mr. Froude, speaking for them and himself. 'Yet perhaps they were forming an opinion prematurely which will hereafter be the verdict of mankind. He, after all, is personally responsible more than any other man for the helpless condition into which the executive administration of the English empire seems to have fallen.' 'Oceana' was published in 1886.

'Gladstone,' writes Professor Fawcett, 'made the speech of the evening. He is a fine speaker. He never hesitates, and his action and manner are admirable. In fact, in this respect he resembles Bright, but is far inferior to Bright, in my opinion, in not condensing his matter. Again, Gladstone is too subtle.' On more than one occasion Fawcett seems to have doubted the judgment of his leader.

Sir E. Watkin writes: 'Sir John A. Macdonald, then Mr. Macdonald, was once taken by me under the gallery, by special order of the Speaker, to hear a great speech of Mr. Gladstone, whom he had not heard before. When we went away I said: "Well, what do you think of him?" He replied: "He is a great rhetorician, but he is not an orator."'

About twenty years ago Mr. Gladstone's future career as a Minister was predicted with singular accuracy by a very acute observer of men and things, who had held almost every possible office, from that of Ministerial Whip to Chancellor of the Exchequer and Secretary of State. Observing from the Peers' Gallery Mr. Gladstone's mismanagement of public business when he led the House of Commons in Lord Russell's short-lived second Administration, he said, in effect: 'We are coming to new times. Mr. Gladstone cannot manage the House of Commons as other Ministers have done, in the usual way, but he can force great measures through by bringing the pressure of outside opinion to bear upon it. This,' he added, 'is the way in which Mr. Gladstone will maintain himself in power. We shall have one violent proposal after another, as the means by which Mr. Gladstone may gain or keep office.'

Mr. John Morley writes: 'He sometimes shows a singular difficulty in apprehending what will be the average judgment even on ordinary proceedings. He showed this in the mistake concerning Sir Robert Collier's hardly more than colourable qualification to be made a member of the Judicial Committee of the Privy Council. He showed it again in a blunder of much the same kind—the special pleader's kind—in the appointment to the Ewelme Rectory of a clergyman who could only by a strained interpretation of the usual rule be regarded as eligible. He showed it more than ever in his attempt to interpret away Lord (then Mr.) Odo Russell's meaning in the language addressed by him in 1870 to Prince Bismarck on the subject of Russia's action concerning the Black Sea clause of the Treaty of Paris, and averring the necessity— England's necessity—for going to war with Russia with or without allies. His hasty resignation of the leadership of the Liberal party in 1874 was a still more important illustration of his rather erratic judgment. The latest instance of it is his letter to Count Carophyl, which shows at the same time, we think, a singularly just appreciation of the diplomatic concessions he had gained, and a singularly inadequate one as to the importance of a proud and lofty tone as one who writes as a spokesman of a great people.'

Mr. Spurgeon, writing to a Cardiff Liberal who opposes Mr. Gladstone's Irish policy, says:

'As to Ireland, I am altogether at one with you; especially I feel the wrong proposed to be done to our Ulster brethren. What have they done to be thus cast off? The whole scheme is as full of dangers and absurdities as if it came from a madman, yet I am sure Mr. Gladstone is only doing justice, and acting for the good of all. I consider him to be making one of those mistakes which can only be made by great and well-meaning men.'

In a further deliverance on the question, 'in answer to many friends,' and expressing himself as sorry to say what he does, liking to agree with Mr. Gladstone, Mr. Spurgeon says:

'We feel bound to express our great regret that the great Liberal leader should have introduced his Irish Bills. We cannot see what our Ulster brethren have done that they should be cast off. They are in great dismay at the prospect of legislative separation from England, and we do not wonder. They have been ever our loyal friends, and ought not to be sacrificed. Surely something can be done for Ireland less ruinous than that which is proposed. The method of pacification now put forward seems to us to be full of difficulties, absurdities, and unworkable proposals. It is well meant, but even the best and greatest may err. We cannot look forward with any complacency to Ulster Loyalists abandoned, and an established Irish Catholic Church, and yet they are by no means the greatest evils which we foresee in the near future, should the suggested policy ever become fact.'

There was a brief intercourse between the two, creditable to each. In 1838 Macaulay writes: 'I found Gladstone in the throng, and I accosted him, as we had never been introduced to each other. He received my advances with very great empressement indeed, and we had a good deal of pleasant chat.'

In 1839 appeared the celebrated work on 'The State in its Relations to the Church.' Macaulay bought it, read it, and wrote to Jeffery: 'The Lord hath delivered him into our hands. I see my way to a popular and at the same time gentleman-like critique.' Again: 'I do think I have disposed of all Gladstone's theories unanswerably, and that there is not a line of the paper even so strict a judge as Sir Robert Inglis would quarrel with as at all indecorous.' Again Macaulay says: 'I have received a letter from Mr. Gladstone, who in generous terms acknowledged, with some reservations, the fairness of the article. "In whatever you write," continues Gladstone, "you can hardly hope for the privilege of most anonymous productions; but if it had been possible not to recognise, I should have questioned your authorship in this particular case, because the candour and single-mindedness which it exhibits are, in one who has long been connected in the most distinguished manner with a political party, so rare as to be almost incredible. . . . In these lacerating times one clings to everything of personal kindness, and husbands it for the future; and if you will allow me, I shall earnestly desire to carry with me such a recollection of your mode of dealing with a subject on which the attainment of truth, we shall agree, materially depends on the temperament in which the search for it is instituted and conducted."' 'How much,' writes Macaulay's biographer, 'this letter pleased Macaulay is evident by the fact of his having kept it unburned, a compliment which, except in this single instance, he never paid to any of his correspondents.' 'I have seldom,' he writes, in reply to Mr. Gladstone, 'been more gratified than by the very kind note which I have just received from you. Your book itself, and everything that I have heard about you—though almost all my information came, I must say, to the honour of our troubled times, from people very strongly opposed to you in politics—led me to regard you with respect and goodwill.' Again Macaulay wrote: 'I have no idea that he will ever acquire the reputation of a great statesman. His views are not sufficiently profound or enlarged for that.'

In 1853 Mrs. Beecher-Stowe, the far-famed author of 'Uncle Tom's Cabin,' was in London, and dined with Mr. Gladstone at the Duke of Argyll's. She writes: 'He is one of the ablest and best men in the kingdom. It is a commentary on his character that, although one of the highest of the High Church, we have never heard him spoken of among the Dissenters otherwise than as an excellent and highly-conscientious man. For a gentleman who has attained such celebrity, both in politics and theology, he looks remarkably young. He is tall, with dark hair and eyes, a thoughtful, serious cast of countenance, and is easy and agreeable in conversation.'

When the Commercial Treaty with France was being discussed, Cobden wrote: 'Gladstone is really almost the only Cabinet Minister of five years' standing who is not afraid to let his heart guide his head a little at times.' In 1860 Cobden wrote to Bright: 'I have told you before that Gladstone shows much heart in this business. . . . He has a strong aversion to the waste of money on our armaments. He has no class feeling about the services. It is a pity that you cannot avoid hurting his feelings by such sallies. . . . He has more in common with you and me than any other man of his power in Britain.' Again: 'I agree with you that Gladstone overworks himself. But I suspect that he has a conscience, which is at times a troublesome partner for a Cabinet Minister. I make allowances for him, for I have never yet been able to define to my own satisfaction how far a man with a view to utility ought to allow himself to be merged in a body of men called a Government, or how far he should preserve his individuality.' In 1862 Mr. Cobden writes: 'Then Gladstone lends his genius to all sorts of expenditure which he disapproves, and devises schemes for raising money which nobody else would think of.' Cobden's last reference to Gladstone seems to have been at the time of the Danish War, when he once more laments the fact that Palmerston was still Premier and able to use all parties for his ends. Cobden writes: 'With Gladstone and Gibson for his colleagues, and with a tacit connivance from a section of the Tories, there can be no honesty in our party life.'

In an 'Essay on the British Parliament' a writer gives the prize of eloquence to Mr. Gladstone. It is, as he truly says, 'Eclipse first, and the rest nowhere.'

'Mr. Gladstone is an appreciated man, but he is not understood. Why not? The first duty of a pretty woman, it has been said, is to let everyone know that she is pretty. Extending that kind of code to the other sex, it is surely the first duty of an intellectual man to be intelligible. In this age there is more of the suspicion that Mr. Gladstone is Talleyrandizing, and using his copious vocabulary for the concealment of thought. . . . He sees so much to say on all sides that he never clearly defines on which side lies the preponderating reasoning. He sums up controversies, rather than ranges himself in them. Debate is with him pure debate—a division appears, in his apprehension, rather to disfigure the proceedings. . . . If Premier himself, he could ally himself on one hand with Mr. Milner Gibson, and on the other with Mr. Spencer Walpole. He is the juste milieu of the day, and, biding his time, he offers to his contingent supporters "chameleon's diet—eating the air promise-crammed."'—'Political Portraits,' by E. M. Whittey, published in 1851, p. 226.

Mr. Hill, in his 'Political Portraits,' writes: 'If Mr. Gladstone has to make up his mind while he is on his legs whether he will or will not answer a delicate question, he will express himself somewhat after this fashion: "The honourable gentleman, in the exercise of that discretion which I should be the last to deny to any member of this House, least of all to one so justly entitled to respect as my hon. friend, both on account of his high personal character and his long Parliamentary experience, has asked me whether the Government intend to bring in a Bill for the establishment of secular education in Ireland. Now, the discretion which I freely concede to the hon. gentleman in regard to the proposal of this question, I must, as a member of the Government, reserve to myself in considering whether or how I shall answer the question. I have to consider it not only in itself, but in regard to the time at which it is put, and the circumstances which surround the topic." Mr. Gladstone then, perhaps, will say, what Lord Palmerston and Lord Russell would have said in a single sentence, that he must decline to answer it.'

Count Beust said: 'Independently of the demerits and dangers of Mr. Gladstone's Home Rule scheme, he has, to my mind, little or no excuse for introducing it, and the parallel he draws between it and the dual system I inaugurated is utterly fallacious. Agrarian agitation is the plea which he uses for giving the Irish people a separate Parliament. I believe that the agrarian system in Ireland has for centuries been a bad one, and the land legislation of 1881—whatever people may think of it from a moral point of view—will unquestionably bring about good results. But how these results are to be beneficially increased by giving Ireland a separate Parliament, and handing over its government to the avowed enemies of England, I cannot see, for one of its first acts would be to pass laws—virtually decrees of expulsion—against the landlords, to banish capital from the land, and materially to aggravate the general condition of the peasantry. As an old statesman, I should consider that the establishment of an Irish Parliament, raising, as it unquestionably would, aspirations on the part of the people to free themselves from the English yoke, and increasing the power of political agitators, is fraught with the gravest danger to England. I cannot understand Mr. Gladstone quoting Austria-Hungary as an example, for, independently of the great dissimilarity between the two systems, Mr. Gladstone forgets the condition of Austria when the Hungarian Parliament was established. Austria had been beaten after a short but most disastrous war; Prussia had forbidden her any further interference in German affairs; the country was almost in a state of latent revolution; and an outbreak in Hungary, promoted by foreign agents and foreign gold, with Klapka doing Count Bismarck's bidding, was in the highest degree probable, and would, had it occurred, have led to almost overwhelming disaster. Knowing this, I felt bound to advise the Emperor to accede to the views of the Déak party, securing the solidarity of the empire by the guarantees afforded through the systems of delegations and joint budget. Mr. Gladstone cannot urge upon your House of Commons the same reasons for granting Home Rule to Ireland. England has not been, and I trust never will be, beaten as Austria had been beaten. No foreign foe has been dictating terms at the gates of London. No revolution is latent, and, a point also worthy of consideration, the population of Ireland is only about five millions, including those Protestants who are against the Home Rule scheme, as compared with what I should think was the wish of the great majority of the thirty millions composing the population of Great Britain; whereas the area of Hungary is greater than that of Austria proper, and its population is nearly one-half of the total population of the empire.'

Well might Count Beust ask: 'How can Mr. Gladstone use my dualistic system as a precedent for his scheme of Home Rule?'

Mr. Joseph Cowen said: 'The super-subtlety of his intellect, his faculty for hair-splitting, and his love of party warfare, create distrust, and generate that strong sense of resentment which exists towards him amongst a numerous section of the community. If he were not so subtle he would be more successful. A plain straight man like Lord Hartington, or Lord John Russell, or Sir Stafford Northcote, impresses the average Englishman more favourably than a curiously acute one like the Prime Minister. The popular impression—that he is an austere purist, and would not resort to any of the tricks or wriggles that characterize ordinary party leaders—is altogether a mistake. Those who are brought in contact with the Legislature know that he can resort to any of the devices of partizanship as readily as men who are popularly accounted his inferiors. It is this many-sidedness that leads to the different estimates that are formed of him.

He cannot but have felt very keenly the death of Gordon, and the massacre that ensued on the fall of Khartoum; yet I believe it is true that he went to the Criterion that night to see a very second-rate comedy. Ordinary persons having the responsibility that he had would not have been able to attend a theatre at such a time. The other day he laboured to impress the House of Commons with the extreme gravity of the position of affairs with Russia, and shortly after he went to see Miss Anderson play in "Pygmalion and Galatea." These sudden changes from seriousness to seeming frivolity foster that sense of distrust which a large number of sober Englishmen feel towards him. They cannot understand how a man engaged in such grave and weighty transactions can feel them very acutely when he can so easily throw them on one side and ignore the responsibilities they entail.'

'What a wonderful fellow Gladstone is, after all!' said Mr. Disraeli one day to McCullagh Torrens. 'He had a dreadful passage, I hear, coming back from Ireland, and the moment he got on shore he began to make a speech to the Welshmen, telling them that they were all right, and to keep so.'

'What an ardent creature!' he exclaimed as Mr. Gladstone rushed past them to vote on another occasion when a division had been called for.

Under the date of June 8, 1885, Sir Stafford Northcote writes: 'The great debate came off to-night. . . . The result, a majority of twelve against Government, took the House greatly by surprise, though we ourselves had reckoned on a victory by three or four votes. About forty of the Parnellites went with us. The excitement on the declaration of the numbers was very great, and displayed itself rather indecorously. Randolph Churchill jumped upon his seat and stood waving his pocket-handkerchief and shouting; Walter left the House with Algernon West, and said something about this being a curious end of Gladstone's career. West said: "Oh, this won't be the end now; you will see him come out more energetic than ever."' Sir Stafford Northcote, it may be stated, seems at times to have been a good deal bothered by Mr. Gladstone. 'The most incredulous man I ever met!' he writes in his diary; 'keeps on shaking his head whenever I refer to him.' Again he writes: 'Gladstone had been dining out to meet the authoress of "Sister Dora"—Miss Lonsdale—who was very much alarmed by the rapidity and variety of his questions.' Again we find him complaining of Gladstone's habit of speaking late into the dinner-hour, so that his opponent must either speak to empty benches or forego the advantage of replying on the instant. After this, we must admit Mr. Gladstone's description of himself on one occasion as an 'old Parliamentary hand.'

'Mr. Gladstone Close at Hand' is the title of Dr. Parker's article of gossip about Mr. Gladstone in the New Review. Once during his last Premiership Dr. Parker had the honour of breakfasting with Mr. Gladstone in Downing Street. After the meal Mr. Gladstone took down a book and read aloud an account of the circumstances under which Ireland was united to Great Britain. The account was so pathetic that the reader broke down and sobbed like a child. The ex-Premier permitted himself to be interviewed by means of a written catechism Dr. Parker sent him, and the answers are given in the article. Perhaps the way in which some of the questions are ingeniously not answered is as instructive as the direct replies to others. Asked whether, in his opinion, the

Church of England had a firmer hold upon the people than ever it had, he said the Church suffered much from the general decline of what is called the prestige of churches, but had gained much from the transformation of the clergy. He does not believe in the interchange of pulpits. 'With all respect for those clergymen who are willing to preach in Nonconformist pulpits, I must say,' he replied, 'they do not seem to form a proper conception of their own Church.'

Dr. Parker, not content with prose, broke out on one occasion into song, as follows:

Lord Hatherley wrote in 1855: 'There is but one man of genius in the House, I think—Gladstone.'

Professor Tyndall wrote in a letter to the Times: 'Nature, which has so richly endowed him in many ways, has denied him the faculty of discerning the defeat which, even in the springtide of power and in the flush of victory, he has over and over again gratuitously wooed. In fact, he thinks too highly of himself and too meanly of his followers. Like Napoleon's generals, they are to him mere mud, to be shaped and moulded according to his imperial will. The dissatisfaction arising from his conduct is not a thing of yesterday. God, as Mahomed says, has made men to be men—not foxes and wolves; and the love of truth and abhorrence of untruth inherent in the healthy British character have gradually opened the eyes of Mr. Gladstone's most able and most independent supporters to his misdeeds. His errors of judgment, his political dishonesty, his impulsiveness and passion, so often invoked for purposes both ungenerous and unwise, his tampering for party ends with the sustaining bulwarks of the State, his cruel indifference to the fate of men far nobler than himself who had trustfully accepted from him tasks the faithful prosecution of which led them to a doom which he might have averted, but did not avert, the voice of many a brother's blood crying from the ground, had already shaken the faith of honest Liberals in their idol, when his flagitious Irish policy put an end to their forbearance and caused them to fling abroad the banner of revolt. The cream of the Liberal party have been the seceders here; the men who above all others adorned the Liberal ranks have been the first to renounce the heresies of their recreant leader. A former worshipper of the ex-Prime Minister said to me some time ago: "Never in the history of England was there such a consensus of intellect arrayed against a statesman as that now arrayed against Mr. Gladstone. What a fall!" . . . I see with concern letters from Liberal Unionists in the Times which seem to indicate that the writers only deem it necessary for Mr. Gladstone to declare his abandonment of Home Rule to make all right again with the Liberals. But who is to guarantee Mr. Gladstone's good faith in this matter? He apostatized, for party purposes, when he became a Home Ruler, and he will apostatize again whenever it suits his ambition to do so. I should not be surprised if, some fine day, he took those simple Unionists at their word and made the required declaration. But could we be sure of him afterwards? For years, according to his own confession, he nourished in the dark corners of his mind this fungus of Home Rule, while to all his friends he seemed earnestly bent on extirpating it. A man of this stamp has no claim to the trust or credence of Liberal Unionists.'

Writing in 1879, Principal Tulloch says: 'I bought the Observer on my way back, and read Gladstone's philippic against the Government. What a man he is! What avenging and concentrated passion and power of hatred at the age of seventy! If he gets back to power, he will certainly play the devil with something.'

Dr. Talmage, who visited Mr. Gladstone at Hawarden a year or two since, sailed from Liverpool on the following day on his return to America. While in the Holy Land he secured a large stone from Calvary, which is intended to form the corner-stone of his proposed new church in Brooklyn. Dr. Talmage, who was interviewed after his visit to Hawarden, said he found Mr. Gladstone hale and hearty, and he ran up and down the hills like a boy. The ex-Premier was sanguine that his Home Rule scheme would succeed. Dr. Talmage asked if his faith in Christianity had wavered in his old age. Mr. Gladstone answered: 'The longer I live, the stronger grows my faith in God, and my only hope for the world is that the human race will be brought more into contact with Divine revelation.'

Mr. Mozley writes in his 'Reminiscences': 'As for Mr. Gladstone, I have for many years seldom thought of him without being reminded of the terrible lines in which Horace describes one of the attendants of that fickle goddess whom he believed to be the arbiter of civil strife. Often have I felt that I would rather grow cabbage, like Cincinnatus, than be the public executioner of usurpations, monopolies, and other abuses. But, after indulging in the sentiment, I have swelled the triumph of justice, peace, and public good. I have generally been so unfortunate in the use of my electoral privileges that I have come to think them hardly worth the fuss made about them; but the most unfortunate use I ever made of them—so I felt at the time— was when I went up to Oxford to vote for Mr. Gladstone, and he was actually elected. It was some excuse for this ridiculous inconsistency that I scarcely ever looked into Mr. Gladstone's weekly organ—of course, he had not a weekly organ in any other sense than he had a tail to his coat—without seeing some very offensive and utterly untrue allusion to myself. . . . But now, what is the singular good fortune or providential protection I began with? Simply this: I never in all my life once saw Mr. Gladstone, from the morning I met him in Hurdis Lushington's room, three or four days after his arrival from Eton, till he was so good as to ask me to breakfast in June, 1882, and kindly suggest an alteration in my book. On the former occasion he had all the purple bloom and freshness of boyhood and the glow of generous emotion.'

Mr. Samuel Morley, M.P., wrote: 'I regard Mr. Gladstone as the greatest, purest, and ablest statesman of the present age, and of all ages or of any age. How great the sympathy during his recent illness throughout the whole civilized world! With what? Not with Mr. Gladstone as M.P. for Midlothian; not with Gladstone as Premier or statesman; but simply with Gladstone as the embodiment of the highest and purest aspirations of that patriotism which desires the best of all good things for the greatest number of our own fellow-countrymen, and that the countrymen of all other countries may partake in these good things also. His life, his health, his genius, his power, and influence are of more consequence to the country than all or any of the most pressing questions now before Parliament.'

No one, as was to be expected, has been more variously or idiotically censured or blamed than Mr. Gladstone. Considerable ingenuity has been displayed by more than one pious clergyman to show that he is the beast of Revelation. In the opinion of one of them—the Rev. Canon Crosthwaite, of Kildare—beheading is too good for Mr. Gladstone. He has 'bamboozled the

House of Commons, and has persuaded it to rob God and put His patrimony into the Treasury of England. Essex lost his head for only talking to O'Neal across the river. What does not Mr. Gladstone deserve,' asks the Canon, in the National Review, 'for trafficking with Irish rebels and betraying to them all the rights of the British Crown? Yet this spoiler of the Church is allowed to read lessons.' Another reverend, possibly a Dissenter, wrote to Mr. Gladstone to suggest that he would add to the services he has rendered religion by conducting a series of services in the Agricultural Hall. In reply, declining the suggestion, Mr. Gladstone wrote: 'It would expose me, with justice, to that charge of ostentation which some think already attaches to me.'

Actually a reverend gentleman compiled, under the head of 'Musical Evenings with the Great and Good,' a service of song. The directions are to open with the hymn, 'Hark, my soul! it is the Lord.' A footnote informs us that 'this hymn of Cowper's has been translated by Mr. Gladstone into Italian.' The direct bearing of these facts is not at once apparent, but possibly enlightenment may arrive during the 'Prayer' which is to follow. The first verse of the next hymn runs:

Later on a kind of parenthetic observation runs, that 'Oxford is an ancient seat of learning, and may be the fountain of intellectual light; but it has ever been the home of political darkness and the defender of exclusive privilege.' As Mr. Gladstone's earlier political career is very sweepingly condemned, and the evil influences of the University deplored, it is to be presumed that the half-century of harvest is a small stretch of the exuberant poetic licence that Mr. Thoseby permits himself occasionally. Personal encouragement to Mr. Gladstone, however, is not wanting, and he is told to

A subsequent song informs him positively that

And that there is to be

But perhaps the climax of Gladstonolatry is reached in the following passages:

'In Mr. Gladstone's work as legislator and administrator there is, from first to last, the same thoroughness and mastery. He never introduced a measure into the House in a crude and incomplete manner. He mastered every detail, and knew exactly the value and bearing of every suggestion and amendment offered, and whether he could admit it or not. He introduced no measures merely to curry favour, to strengthen his party, or catch the popular vote. He has always had regard to pressing needs, and has made it a matter of duty to press and pass the measures he introduced. And these measures have never been condemned except by "politicians in distress." In his work as administrator he has not left the work to be done by subordinates. He has attended to his own duties, and toiled to understand every particular, and, in consequence, he has never had to vacillate, taking a position to-day from which he has had to withdraw to-morrow; saying one thing to-day and contradicting it the next.'

Remarkable as is the polished literary style of this citation, it is surpassed in the following fantastic rhapsody:

'His beautiful residence at Hawarden Castle, in Cheshire, has much of the old baronial associations connected with it. It is delightfully situated in a finely-wooded park, where Mr. Gladstone's well-known penchant for tree-felling, as a relaxation, finds ample scope. And where he also may gaze with joy on hill and dale, and

And where, perchance, he may now and again sing to the birds. Might not those birds, those beautiful birds, represent Freedom! Political Freedom, the Sovereignty of Ideas, the Monarchy of Mind, the Republic of Intellect, Free Thought, Free Speech, Free Pews, Free Churches in a Free State, until there shall be no Party but God, and no Politics but Religion—the mighty Christ all in all.'

In 1870 Mr. Grant Duff, in the course of one of his addresses to his constituents, said that some years ago, when Mr. Gladstone's Administration was in power, a clever Tory, who hated both Mr. Gladstone and his Administration, wrote the following acrostic:

This acrostic was repeated in a drawing-room in the presence of a young lady of good Liberal principles, and the daughter of a well-known Member of Parliament, who, without leaving the room, went to a table and wrote this answer to it:

The bitterness of some of the attacks on Mr. Gladstone were at any rate a great testimony to his surpassing power and popularity. In 1880 appeared a handbill under the title of the 'Gladstonian Mess,' announcing: 'A grand banquet will be given at the Boar's Head Hotel immediately after the sale of the effects of Mr. John Bull, previously announced, carefully prepared by Mr. W. E. Gladstone, the auctioneer, and at the vendor's expense, to which all the company are invited.' The sale was announced—Mr. Gladstone the auctioneer: 'The whole of the vast landed estates, goods, chattels and effects of Mr. John Bull, who is retiring from business on account of advancing age and ill-health, induced by recent losses in the Transvaal venture, comprising three kingdoms (united or otherwise), one empire, one dominion, forty-eight colonies, and one Suzerainty, one large public-house, known as the Lords and Commons, also an extremely elegant, spacious, and well-built family residence, known as the Buckingham Palace, with greenhouses, gardens, stables, and every necessary appointment. The residence contains ample accommodation for a family of position, is situate in its own grounds, and commands good views of the Nelson Monument, St. Paul's Cathedral, and Westminster Abbey, and is within easy distance of the thriving market towns of London and Westminster.' As an indication, on the other hand, of Mr. Gladstone's popularity, let me refer to the Gladstone claret, which was supposed to be a peculiarly economical and refreshing beverage, and the Gladstone travelling-bag, which was described as a bag adapted for the requirements of all travellers, of all ages, of both sexes and in all grades of life. Someone took the trouble to issue the prospectus of what was called the Gladstone Exploitation Company, a further unintentional tribute.

The following appeared in a Turkish newspaper at the time of the Bulgarian atrocities: 'Mr. Gladstone is of Bulgarian descent. His father was a pig-dealer in the villayet of Kusteridje. Young Gladstone ran away at the age of sixteen to Servia, and was then with another pig-dealer sent to London to sell pigs. He stole the proceeds, changed his name from Troradin to Gladstone, and became a British subject. Fortune favoured him till he became Prime Minister. Gladstone has no virtues. Gold is his god. The Ottoman Government offered him five thousand pounds to put their finances in order, but subsequently withdrew the offer, and his vexation at this, combined with his bad Bulgarian nature, caused his opposition to the Turks. The surname "Gladstone" means lust for gold, and was given to him on account of his failings in that respect.'

In the 'Life of Lord Houghton' we find another illustrative anecdote. The writer says: 'One day, a few years before his death, when he was dining at the house of Mr. James Knowles, the conversation turned upon the relative characteristics of Mr. Gladstone and Lord Beaconsfield, and it was remarked by someone that if Lord Beaconsfield was a good judge of men, Mr. Gladstone was a still better judge of mankind. Houghton was asked to turn the epigram into verse, and he did it as follows:

In connection with these great men it is interesting to note that in 1867, when Parliament met, Mrs. Disraeli was lying seriously ill. Mr. Gladstone, in the opening sentence of his speech on the Address, gave public expression to the sympathy of all parties. Lord Houghton, in referring to the fact, adds: 'The scene in the House of Commons was very striking; Dizzy quite unable to restrain his tears.' When Lord Beaconsfield died, however, many were found to censure Mr. Gladstone for not having been present at the funeral of his distinguished rival.

Lord Blachford's letters contain many short notices of Mr. Gladstone. In 1858 he gives a sketch of him in a conference with Sir Edward Bulwer: 'It was very absurd to see them talking it over; Gladstone's clear, dark eye and serious face, and ponderous forehead and calm manner, was such a contrast with Sir E.'s lean and narrow face and humid, theatrical, conscious kind of ways.' In 1868 he writes to Newman: 'I have not yet got through Gladstone's autobiography. . . . Of course, as you say, some of his friends think it injudicious, and I am not sure that it is not injudicious on that very account. One great weight which Gladstone has to carry in the political race is a character for want of judgment, and every addition to that is an impediment.' In 1874, in July, when Mr. Gladstone appeared in Parliament after four months' absence to oppose the Bill for the Abolition of Church Patronage in Scotland, Lord Blachford writes: 'Gladstone's opposition is curious. I am sorry to say I cannot go with him on either of his points—indeed, I may almost say on any. I see no reason why the Scotch Church should not have their way about patronage. I think the cry against the Public Worship Bill a scare, and I particularly object to the principle and working of the Endowed Schools Act. However, everybody seems to agree that he made a great speech on the Public Worship Bill as a matter of oratory. He does not seem to care much about what was his party, who, I suppose, are dead against him on two out of three of these points.'

Of Mr. Gladstone, John Arthur Roebuck, a bellicose Radical—very noisy in his time—says: 'He may be a very good chopper, but, depend upon it, he is not an English statesman.' Of Tennyson, it is said that he loved Mr. Gladstone, but detested his policy.

The late Sir James Stansfeld is reported as saying to an interviewer: 'Mr. Gladstone's conduct in the Cabinet was very curious. When I first joined in 1871, I naturally expected that his position was so commanding that he would be able to say, "This is my policy; accept it or not, as you like." When Sir James Graham was examined before a committee on Admiralty administration, he was asked: "What would happen if a member of your Board did not agree with your policy?" He answered: "He would cease to be a member of my board." I thought Mr. Gladstone would have taken the same line, but he did not. He was always profuse in his expressions of respect for his Cabinet. There is a wonderful combination in Mr. Gladstone of imperiousness and deference; in the Cabinet he would assume that he was nothing.'

In the Nineteenth Century appeared a curious estimate of Mr. Gladstone by an Indian gentleman. 'He has,' he writes, 'a natural prejudice, almost antipathy, to the name of Turk. His mind, in some respects, resembles that of some pious, learned, but narrow-minded priest of the middle ages; and his unreasoning prejudice against the Turk is indeed mediæval, and worthy of those dark ages of blood, belief and Quixotic chivalry. A person of such character, however graphic and sublime he may be, should not have such a great political influence on the minds of millions of his fellow-beings; he should not be at the head of a vast empire such as that of England of to-day if he cannot constrain his emotions and his ecclesiastical prejudices. He is a sublime moral leader of men; but a statesman of Mr. Gladstone's position should be more calm, more deliberate, and should weigh his words carefully before he speaks. He should take care that his writings and speeches do not wound the feelings of millions of his fellow-subjects.'

On the defeat of the Liberal party in 1895, the National Review wrote: 'One can now appreciate the previously provoking description of Mr. Gladstone as a great Conservative force. His Irish escapade has shattered the Liberal party, made the House of Lords invulnerable, and the Church unassailable.' Dr. Guinness Rogers wrote that Mr. Gladstone's retirement was one of the causes of the defeat of the Liberal party. 'It is to a large extent a measure of the enormous influence of that commanding personality. Not until the secret history of that period can be studied will it be known how tremendous was the loss which the Liberal party sustained by the withdrawal from the strife of a leader who towered head and shoulders over all his associates.'

Mr. Gladstone seems seldom to have made a speech but his friends favoured him with their criticisms. Thus, when in 1871 he visited Yorkshire and made speeches at Wakefield and Whitby, Lord Houghton wrote, after praising one of his speeches: 'I cannot say as much for your Whitby speech, for it confirmed my feelings that on the high mountain where you stand there is a demon, not of demagogism, but of demophilism, that is tempting you sorely. I am no alarmist, but it is undeniable that a new and thoroughly false conception of the relations of work and wealth is invading society, and of which the Paris Commune is the last expression. Therefore one word from such a man as you, implying that you look on individual wealth as anything else than a reserve of public wealth, and that there can be any antagonism between them, seems to me infinitely dangerous.' Mr. Gladstone replied, writes Lord Houghton's biographer, with his usual frankness and friendliness to the remonstrances of his old friend, 'whose criticisms are marked by the kindly tone which is habitual with you, though I do not agree with everything you say about property.'

Sir Francis Doyle will have it that to Mr. Disraeli is due the fact that Mr. Gladstone left the Conservatives. 'We may all of us recollect,' he writes, 'the Irish soldiers who marched up to and then passed a standard erected by William III. Some regiments moved to the right and others to the left, the right-hand division taking service under Louis XIV., the other division submitting to the English Government. On their first separation they were but an inch or two apart, but the distance gradually widened between them till they or their representatives met face to face at Fontenoy. So, after Sir Robert Peel's death, Lord Beaconsfield's presence established like that standard a line of demarcation between the two portions of the Tory party. Had it not been for the line fixed across their path, I think Mr. Gladstone, Herbert, and the other Peelites would have joined Lord Derby instead of the Whigs. Nor would Mr. Gladstone's logic have been in fault (when is it?), or failed to justify abundantly the course he had taken.'

CHAPTER XVII. AT HOME.

Hawarden Park, in the centre of which stands Hawarden Castle, is one of the finest country seats in the three kingdoms. Visitors who arrive at Hawarden for the first time are surprised at the extent of the grounds and the beauty of the park. Hawarden Park, with Hawarden Castle, came to Mr. Gladstone with his wife. When Mr. Gladstone married he had no intention of making his seat in Wales, but finding that Sir Stephen Glynne was in circumstances which rendered it disadvantageous to the family for him to live in the Castle, Mr. Gladstone bought some of the land, and took up his quarters with his father-in-law in the Castle, which had been temporarily closed. This arrangement lasted for many years, and was attended with none of the disagreeable consequences which so often happen when two generations live under one roof. The two families lived side by side, and nothing could exceed the harmony of the united households. Sir Stephen Glynne always sat at the head of the table, while Mrs. Gladstone sat at the other end; Mr. Gladstone sat between. This arrangement continued down to the death of Sir Stephen Glynne, and it was rather curious to see a statesman whose name and whose fame were familiar throughout the world always taking the second place in his own house. But for the somewhat embarrassed circumstances of Sir Stephen Glynne, which led Mr. Gladstone to buy some of the Glynne estate, it was his intention to have bought a seat in Scotland, to which, as his native country, Mr. Gladstone was always strongly attached. The accident, therefore, of a temporary financial embarrassment on the part of his father-in-law made Hawarden famous throughout the world, and supplied Mr. Gladstone with a very much more convenient country seat than any which he could have procured north of the Tweed.

The Castle is situated on the summit of a range of hills overlooking Chester and the river Dee. The village contains the remains of a castle which dates back almost to the Conqueror, and the ancient mound fortification, the ditch and drawbridge, and the keep, are proof to-day of its power in the past. The old Castle standing in the grounds is scarce more than a relic now. The modern Castle in which the Gladstone family resides was built over a hundred years ago, and has been considerably added to from time to time, so that it is a comparatively new seat. It has a splendid appearance; the stone battlements and walls, which are well grown with ivy, look especially striking. The grounds contain several points of interest, and are exceedingly well wooded, even now, much to the surprise of many visitors, who have heard no little of Mr. Gladstone's powers with his axe.

The new buildings of the Library, which stand not far from the church, have a neat entrance-gate leading to them, with a well-kept lawn on each side. It is in no sense a public institution, but is intended to afford to clergymen and others an opportunity of quiet study. Here are gathered thousands of volumes, carefully selected, representing an eclectic field of thought, including the whole area of human interest. By the side of an erudite Churchman like Pusey you will discover a book by a Nonconformist like Dale. The volumes were in many cases brought to the library by Mr. Gladstone's own hands, and on many an afternoon he was to be seen walking through the park with a bundle of books, to be arranged on the shelves by his own hands or under his superintendence. Not far off in the village street stands the substantial building called the Hawarden Institute. Upstairs in the library are to be seen volumes with characteristic inscriptions by Mr. Gladstone. On the flyleaf of one of the Waverley Novels is written, for instance: 'No library should be complete without a set of Sir Walter Scott's novels in full. Accordingly, I present this set to the Hawarden Institute.' Attached to the institute is a capital billiard-room, a bath-room, and a reading-room. The gymnasium, which was given by Mr. Herbert Gladstone, is not patronized quite so much as that gentleman, it is understood, desires.

The library at Hawarden is one of the finest private libraries in the country. It consists of more than twenty thousand volumes, and considerable curiosity existed as to what Mr. Gladstone intended to do with this collection of books after his death. Contrary to the usual practice obtaining in magnificent private libraries, Mr. Gladstone allowed his books to be lent out to almost anyone in the neighbourhood who wished to read them. At one time this liberty was unlimited; anyone could take a book out and keep it an indefinite period, provided that he simply left an acknowledgment of having borrowed the book. This privilege, however, was so much abused by some persons that a few years ago a rule was laid down limiting the time for which a book might be kept to one month. With that exception, however, the Hawarden Library is still the free loan library of the countryside.

'Within, Hawarden Castle,' says a writer in the World, 'though not ambitiously large, contains more than one roomy cell for its scholar-recluse. At every corner the signs of taste and culture abound. The pictures have been only slightly thinned by the handsome contribution to the Wrexham Exhibition, and curious china is not entirely absent. Oriental jars and costly cabinets of Japanese lacquer are scattered about the handsome rooms with tasteful carelessness, and here and there are specimens of art needlework, in the revival of which Mrs. Gladstone is known to take great interest. But the peculiarity of the house is the vast flood of books, which no one apartment can contain. Out of one library into another, and into drawing-room and dining-room, books have flowed in a resistless stream, pushing other things aside, and establishing themselves in their place. There are books new and old, rare and common, choice editions and ordinary manuals of reference, ponderous tomes of controversial theology and snappish little pamphlets on the currency, with other equally light and pleasant subjects. Over all reigns that air of easy and natural luxury which forms the principal charm of the English country-house proper, as distinguished from the comfortless vastness of foreign châteaux and the pretentious splendour of the suburban villa of the nouveau riche. The castellan, however, is no admirer of nooks and snuggeries, loving most to get through his morning reading in an especially large apartment, garnished with movable bookshelves—a transparent hive for a working bee—amid abundant air and floods of sunshine. "Air and light," and plenty of them, are among his prime conditions of existence.'

'Mr. Gladstone's study,' says another visitor, 'is rather curiously arranged. The walls are covered with books, and volumes are also massed on large shelves jutting out from the walls into the room. Between each partition of books there is room to walk; thus the saving of space in arranging the library in this manner is enormous. The stock of books perhaps exceeds fifteen thousand volumes, and notwithstanding this large number, Mr. Gladstone has little difficulty in placing his hand upon any volume that he may require. There are three writing-desks in the room; one is chiefly reserved for correspondence of a political nature and another is used by Mrs. Gladstone. Looking out of the study window, the flower-beds facing the Castle present a picturesque appearance, while the heavy-wooded grounds beyond stand out in bold relief.'

The village itself is only one street, and a small one; but no village has become more famous and has been more visited by savants, politicians, famous individuals, foreign or English, and deputations consisting of working men, either to watch the great statesman felling trees or to hear him talk.

In a magazine known as the Young Man appeared a few years since an interesting account of Mr. Gladstone's home life, which may claim to be quoted here. The writer, who was one of Mr. Gladstone's nearest neighbours and most intimate friends, said that there was no home in the United Kingdom where there was more freedom of opinion or more frankness in expressing disagreement than in the home of Mr. Gladstone.

'His daily life at home is a model of simplicity and regularity, and the great secret of the vast amount of work he accomplishes lies in the fact that every odd five minutes is occupied. No man ever had a deeper sense of the preciousness of time and the responsibility which everyone incurs by the use or misuse he makes of it. To such a length does he carry this that at a picnic to a favourite Welsh mountain he has been seen to fling himself on the heather, and bury himself in some pamphlet upon a question of the day, until called to lighter things by those who were responsible for the provision basket. His grand maxim is never to be doing nothing.

'Although Mr. Gladstone's daily routine is familiar to some, yet many inaccurate accounts have been circulated from time to time. In bed about twelve, he sleeps like a child until called in the morning. Not a moment's hesitation does he allow himself, although, as we have heard him say, no schoolboy could long more desperately for an extra five minutes. He is down by eight o'clock, and at church (three-quarters of a mile off) every morning for the 8.30 service. No snow or rain, no tempest, however severe, has ever been known to stop him. Directly after breakfast a selection of his letters is brought to him.

'Excepting before breakfast, Mr. Gladstone does not go out in the morning. At 2 p.m.,' continues the Young Man, 'he comes to luncheon, and at the present time he usually spends the afternoon arranging the books at his new library. To this spot he has already transported nearly twenty thousand books, and every volume he puts into its place with his own hand. To him books are almost as sacred as human beings, and the increase of their numbers is perhaps as interesting a problem as the increase of population. It is real pain to him to see a book badly treated—dropped on the floor, unduly squeezed into the bookcase, dog's-eared, or, worst crime of all, laid open upon its face.

'A short drive or walk before the social cup of tea enables him to devote the remaining hour or so before post-time to completing his correspondence. After dinner he returns to his sanctum—a very temple of peace in the evening, with its bright fire, armchair, warm curtains, and shaded reflecting candle. Here, with an occasional doze, he reads until bedtime, and thus ends a busy, fruitful day. Mr. Gladstone has often been heard to remark that had it not been for his Sunday rest, he would not now be the man he is. Physically, intellectually, and spiritually, his Sunday has been to him a priceless blessing. From Saturday night to Monday morning Mr. Gladstone puts away all business of a secular nature, keeps to his special Sunday books and occupations, and never dines out that day unless to cheer a sick or sorrowful friend.'

Hawarden Castle was much improved after passing into Mr. Gladstone's hands. In commemoration of the golden wedding the porch in front of the Castle was erected, a building that adds much to its appearance. A writer in Harper's Magazine says: 'A glance over the tables in the drawing-room at Hawarden Castle leads one to the conviction that Mr. Gladstone is the most photographed man in the world. The tables are literally covered with photographs presenting the well-known face and figure in all habitual circumstances and attitudes. Mr. Gladstone submits to the photographer much upon the same principle that he endures many other of the experiences that sadden life. He recognises a certain amount of possession that the public have in him, and if they insist upon taking it out in photography, that is their affair. He is not only photographed often, but happily, having, indeed, by this time acquired so much skill that he always comes out well. But,' continues the writer, 'no photograph, or the fine oil painting of Millais, comes up to the interest possessed by a little ivory painting which lies in the drawing-room at Hawarden. It represents a little boy some two years of age sitting on the knee of a little girl in nymph-like costume, and fondly supposed to be learning his letters. He has, in truth, one chubby little finger pointed towards the book which rests on his sister's knees, but his face is raised, and two great brown eyes look inquiringly into those of the beholder. This is the child— the father of the man who sits in the other room, though beyond the measurement of the floor there stretches between them the long span of seventy years. The little girl is Mr. Gladstone's sister, who died. The portrait was taken in Liverpool, while Mr. John Gladstone lived in Rodney Street.

'Mr. Gladstone has recently disposed of the question of his hobbies. He has none. Before the day of his retirement into private life, however, the public took a partially proprietary interest in what they were pleased to consider his hobby of cutting down trees.

'It became so notorious that foreigners got to suppose that Mr. Gladstone did little else in his spare time but fell timber, and Americans who visited Hawarden Castle were disappointed at not finding the park a desolation of tree-stumps.

'That Mr. Gladstone should often have gone out, axe in hand, to assist his woodmen was really the most natural thing imaginable. Wood-cutting was just the kind of Titanic exercise in which he delighted to let out the flood of his energy. Again, the park being one of the best timbered in England, it was to be expected that Mr. Gladstone, with a keen eye to the improvement of the property, should take a personal interest in the removal of those trees whose growth, position or decay marred the splendour of their neighbours.

'Mr. Gladstone is now a very old man—older than many who remember him in his vigorous Parliamentary days quite realize. It is many years since his wood-cutting exploits. But, three summers ago, on a special occasion, he went out for the last time on his favourite pastime. The axe that he used—a new one, and lighter than those he usually wielded—is now stored away in a cupboard in Mr. Herbert Gladstone's room at the Castle. "To the end of the handle," says a writer in Pearson's Magazine for March, "is pasted a little label with the brief inscription:

'Mr. Gladstone's favourite implement was the ordinary wedge-shaped American axe. But one that he used a great deal in later days still stands in a corner of his study. Its long, thin blade made it a difficult weapon to handle skilfully; yet the shape or size of the axe made little difference to so experienced a craftsman. In an outdoor room at Hawarden, now chiefly devoted to the storage of bicycles and fishing-baskets, are between thirty and forty axes piled together—long axes and short axes, thick and thin, plain and varnished, new and worn. These represent only a small portion of the collection that Mr. Gladstone once had. In bygone days admirers were constantly sending him axes as marks of their esteem, and now other admirers quite as constantly smuggle them away as treasured mementoes of their visits.

'Besides these workaday axes one may see several with silver heads, and among them one, especially valued, that was presented to Mr. Gladstone in 1884 by the workmen on the Forth Bridge. There are, too, miniature axes beautifully modelled in solid gold, kept among the jewels in the drawing-room; and a silver pencil, axe-shaped, which was presented to the G. O. M. by the Princess of Wales "for axing questions."'

In 1870 Hayward writes: 'I had an immensity of talk on all subjects with Gladstone. I strolled about with him for some hours yesterday. He takes whatever work he has to do easily enough here, and finds time for general reading into the bargain.' In 1871 the same writer says: 'Gladstone as he always is as a companion—conversation singularly rich and varied.' Such seems to have been the common testimony of all who had the honour of spending a brief time with Mr. Gladstone at home.

It is idle, and would be tiresome, to give the history of the deputations of working-men who went to Hawarden. As an illustration, let me say that one December day a number of the working-men of Derby went to Hawarden to present Mr. Gladstone with a dessert-service of Derby china, specially manufactured at the Derby Crown Works for the occasion. When in 1882 Mr. Gladstone celebrated his political jubilee, addresses and telegrams came to him at Hawarden from all parts of the country. When in 1877 Hawarden was invaded by fourteen hundred members of the Bolton Liberal Club, he refused to see them, but quietly informed them that he and his son were about to fell a tree in the course of the day in the park, and thither the crowd repaired, where, after Mr. Gladstone had performed his task, he gave them an address. One of his great wood-cutting feats that year was his felling an enormous beech-tree—a task he performed in three hours. It was a tough job, considering that it measured thirteen feet in circumference, and was a good proof of the aged statesman's muscular strength and activity. Hercules alone seems to have been his equal.

Perhaps one of the most enormous deputations ever received at Hawarden was in 1886, when the Irish deputations came over in great strength to Hawarden, one of them bearing an address signed by 600,000 Irish women. The others brought to him the freedoms of Cork, Limerick, Waterford, and Clonmel. In acknowledging the addresses received, Mr. Gladstone dwelt upon the moderation with which the Home Rule agitation was carried on. He declared that it would ultimately succeed, and denied that the Irish demand involved separation. Yet at one time there were fears for Hawarden and Mr. Gladstone. In 1882 Lord Houghton, while staying there, wrote to his son:

Of the Hawarden Post-office a volume might be written. There could scarcely have been one more filled with important correspondence in all the empire. Everyone deemed it to be his duty to pester Mr. Gladstone with letters, and his replies in the shape of postcards were to be found carefully preserved everywhere. Even illness severe and protracted was no excuse. 'One of the most painful incidents connected with Mr. Gladstone's illness,' writes the London correspondent of the Birmingham Daily Post, 'is the persistence of uninvited spiritual advisers in addressing him. I am told that not a day, and scarcely a post, passes without some of these personages intruding themselves.

'Chapters from the Old and New Testaments, the lives of Scriptural personages, isolated texts, hymns and religious books—in some cases the advice coming from the unknown authors themselves—have all been suggested for the veteran statesman's "edification."

'In not a few instances poems on the same theme have been sent for his perusal, and, as the authors have generally put it, for his spiritual comfort and relief. I need hardly say that these effusions have never reached Mr. Gladstone, but they have in not a few instances, by their very suggestiveness of impending disaster, caused distress to his family.'

A representative of the Daily Mail added more on this subject: 'Among people in touch with the Hawarden household it is being discussed with a good deal of indignant comment, and more than one well-known name is mentioned as having been appended to some of this correspondence. It is not so much the gratuitous impertinence of the amateur spiritual consoler which occasions the annoyance Mr. Gladstone's relatives feel.

'Mr. Gladstone has throughout his life loomed so large in the eyes of the religious public that he has always been a favourite target for the controversialists of every sect. He long ago grew accustomed to being bombarded with controversial pamphlets, and to being assailed with texts of Scripture bearing more or less obliquely upon some political question of the day. And whenever he has been suffering from some trifling indisposition, or has sustained any family loss or affliction, sackfuls of letters quoting texts of Scripture have been sent to him. It occasions neither surprise nor any great amount of annoyance, therefore, now that the sympathy of everyone is turned towards him, that in the case of fervid religionists it should find expression in passages of Scripture and extracts from devotional works from which the senders have themselves, in times of sorrow and affliction, derived comfort and consolation.

'But there are other classes of correspondents. There are people who urge him for his soul's sake to see the error of his ways while there is yet time; there are people who see occasion in his present illness to hasten to say that they forgive him for holding theological views differing from their own; there are people who invite him to send a subscription to something with a view to insuring to himself posthumous satisfaction, as well as the advantage of grateful prayer and intercession.

'But, worst of all, and most painful to the relatives to bear, are the frantic efforts of the testimonial hunters in a hurry. One patent medicine has made strenuous endeavours to foist itself upon him, with an obvious view to subsequent advertisement.

'Of course, there is another side to the picture. The kindly and sympathetic messages and inquiries which have come from people of all ranks, from her Majesty the Queen downwards, have been of great comfort.'

I conclude this rapid survey with a quotation from Mr. G. W. E. Russell's 'Gladstone': 'In order to form the highest and truest estimate of Mr. Gladstone's character, it is necessary to see him at home. But to do this is a privilege accorded necessarily to the few. The public can only judge him by his public life; and from this point of view it may be that the judgment of one of his colleagues may be accepted when he said: "The only two things Mr. Gladstone really cares for are the Church and finance."' What may be the verdict of history on him as a statesman it is impossible to foretell. In England, at any rate, no man has been a power so long. To most of us, to borrow from Shakespeare, he seems to bestride this narrow world like a Colossus. He has done much to help the advent of the new democracy, but it is as a commercial reformer, apparently, that Mr. Gladstone will be best known to future ages. In that capacity he produced marvellous changes. By making paper cheap he gave an impulse to the publishing trade, of which we have not yet seen the end. By the Methuen Treaty it was deemed a heavy blow was struck at Portugal. Under Mr. Gladstone, with the aid of Richard Cobden, that treaty was got rid of, the light wines of France were introduced, the social habits of the country were changed for the better, and the commerce of the country largely increased. The anomalies of the navigation laws were perhaps more marvellous than those of the commercial treaties. Mr. Gladstone had much to do with removing those anomalies, and the result was a marvellous increase in the growth of British shipping and foreign commerce, and the revenue increased, as Mr. Gladstone stated, by leaps and bounds; and while the working man has secured better wages, his power of purchase has been largely increased. Alas! poverty, selfishness, ignorance are still at work in our midst, and Utopia seems as far off as ever.

On May 19 the end came, and all over the world, to the grief of the nation, it was known that Mr. Gladstone was no more.

Parliament unanimously voted him a Public Funeral in Westminster Abbey, where he was laid to rest May 28, 1898.

billing and sons, printers. guildford.